The Book Of Origin "Memoirs Of Life"

Victor Dyastinteen

*This book is not just the memoir of my life but the
life of everyone that has been and will ever be
born and eventually pass.*

Dedication

This book is dedicated to my wife, without whom it would not have been possible. I owe a lot to my wife; she taught me what true love means and how life should be lived.

Before meeting my wife, I never told my parents I loved them and never gave them hugs and or kisses because I hadn't experienced those emotions before. Don't get me wrong: my parents loved me as much as they knew how to love and express oneself.

I saw my wife tell her parents she loves them and give them hugs and kisses, so I began doing the same to my parents. I'll never forget the first time I told my mom I loved her. Her eyes widened, and she was speechless until she said "I Love You" back to me.

I lost my mom to cancer when she was just 60 years old, but before her passing, she witnessed my son Cody's 1ST birthday. I took a picture of her holding my son when they were both sleeping. The best picture ever!

I spent years telling my mom and dad how much I loved them, so when I lost her, my heart was at peace knowing that she knew how much I loved her.

My father is 97 years old, and his mind is as sharp as a knife. His wisdom guides me to be well-rounded in my spirituality to give balance to my understanding of science. I hope to live as long as him.

Acknowledgment

To all those who came before me in the exploration of science, it is true when they say knowledge is power. Literally, if we had the knowledge to convert nuclear energy into electrical energy, we would be able to power the entire continent of the United States for 300 years before half of its power is depleted. Now, that is true power, and Mother Nature gave it to us, but we just don't have the knowledge to achieve this goal.

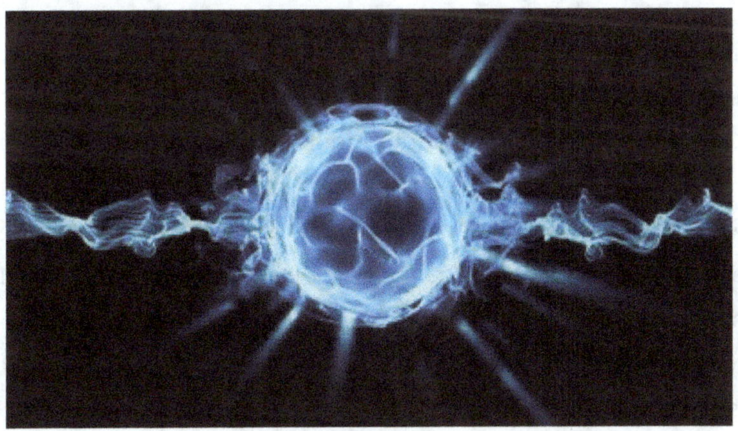

About the Author

I am not a writer per se, but I know that the information that I have acquired over my decades of life has a great potential to help others in their quest for self-discovery.

I am a born adventurer, explorer, scientist, and creator. I love spending time in nature, be it camping, hiking, skiing, or swimming, anything that keeps me active and experiencing life to its fullest.

Being the way I am, I had to know everything, like how radio waves work and how those same waves can be turned into a picture with sound on a TV, but I found out the hard way not to work with something that you have no knowledge of. As a young fellow obsessed with science, I wanted to find a substance where electrons can flow freely, so when electricity is applied, it could move from one point to the other with no resistance because resistance creates heat and any power source that's by-product is heat is waste and not efficient.

So, I came up with a theory to make what I called carbonic gas, a medium with free electrons; it was a mixture of carbon and mixed acid with an anode and cathode with voltage applied in a vacuum. Low and behold to my ambitiousness, I observed the arcs in the bottom of the container with white clouds of billowing smoke appearing, and it was increasing; for a second, I thought that my dreams had come true until my container exploded at the kitchen table, my ears were ringing, my hand was stinging. I could have lost my life, eyes, or hands, but the angels were watching over me. I still hear the vibration of my Dad yelling at me; I felt like Charlie Brown when he would hear the adults talk; I couldn't really hear anything for 30 minutes or so. So, never again shall I be unprepared for my future experiments; I spent several years obtaining knowledge that allowed me to see the connection that binds us all together with our surroundings, knowledge that allows me to see the inner workings of the atomic structure and its true potential.

I believe that my experience with spirituality and science gave me the opportunity to admire the connection we all share with our surroundings, which led to the creation of The Book of Origin, "Memoirs of Life," to help explain to others what I discovered, and for those willing to listen may find the key to their salvation for the here and now, and our purpose in life, so we can prepare for what's to come.

Everything you read in this book is a true account of my life and experiences; some things that I could not explain before this book now fall in line with the references in this book. Remember, according to "Occam's razor," when all other possibilities are explained, then whatever the simplest explanation is must be true.

So, I hope the information in this book can help you as much as it helped me because this book is not just my memoir but yours as well.

Preface

The Book of Origin is an informational guide to help individuals such as yourself understand the meaning of life and the purpose of your existence. It will address aspects like love at first sight, why we fall in love with someone we just met and the science behind it. How can we hate somebody but not really know the reasons why?

Why sometimes do we feel sad, alone, and depressed? Basically, why do we feel all the emotions that we feel?

The what, why, and how of this winding river that we call life, which is sometimes tranquil and at other times turbulent, will be answered with the help of science as we know it. Thorough elucidation of all the common walks of life will be done in The Book of Origin to help others extend their boundaries of belief, understanding, and self-worth.

So, I hope that when you are done with this book, it opens your eyes to ample possibilities you could never have resorted to because you simply didn't know of them. Perhaps this book will give you a better understanding of yourself so you can have a more fulfilling life.

Looking at my life and experiences, I have concluded that it is always easier to turn around and away from matters of life. To simply look the other way and do nothing is easy. If you don't stand for something, then you will fall for anything.

On the other hand, it is hard to stand up and do the right thing for yourself and for others. It is hard for anyone and everyone.

There was a point in my life where I took whatever I wanted. The world was my oyster, and everything was at my disposal: money, power, etc. Whatever I wanted, I got it, but it all came at a price. There is a price for everything that you must pay. It depends on how far you are willing to go. Have you got it in you? What does it take to get what you want.? Are you ready to give all you have got to get what your heart desires? These are the questions you need to ask yourself first.

It all comes down to how far and how much; that's the question you need to ask yourself. Doing nothing won't get you anything, but while taking that hard step of going the farthest, of risking it all to attain your dreams, you must remember that there is no coming back from certain places– places that are so dark at times that they will trap you, consume you and devour you completely.

At some point in my life, I started to try to do the right thing. That's when I learned that I felt empowered whenever I helped others. Helping others gave me happiness and positive energy I hadn't experienced. The sense of empowerment, happiness, and energy that came with it made me feel like I was doing the right thing in helping others. Perhaps this is my purpose. The fruits of the seed I had once planted in me pushed me to continue serving my purpose.

I started to see the bigger picture and became aware of my purpose in life, but I knew I must tread carefully because once something is done, sooner or later, it could have consequences that I don't want any part of. Because knowledge and technology that is not shared is a waste, but technology shared and abused could have catastrophic events impacting millions; just ask J. Robert Oppenheimer, Max Born, David Bohm, and others.

Therefore, rather than putting all my eggs in one basket and grabbing for the golden ring, I started to find other avenues to obtain my life goals. This book is one of many such routes that I have stumbled upon in funding my purpose in life. I have seen many people go through life and not know who they are or what they are supposed to do with their lives—billions of people before you and me have lived and died just like that. Perhaps billions will live and die in the same manner, never obtaining their true potential, never getting to know themselves, never fulfilling their purpose in life.

While navigating through life, I found out that the more I observed my surroundings, the more I could see the trail that was laid out for me that I needed to follow.

The more I listened to my inner spirit and sense of direction, the more a path would unveil itself to me by leaving unsubtle signs here and there. Therefore, I believe everything is always right in front of you; you just need to be willing to look for it. Your guiding force will take you to it if only you befriend it. Ignoring it or going against it will only do you harm.

Everyone has an internal sense of direction that guides them in life and takes them places. I am of the viewpoint that when you fear to follow your sense of direction, negative things start to happen. Some people call it bad luck, but I call those signs that need to be validated by making changes until you start to feel positive emotion and happiness.

Those are the signs that determine that you are on the right path. Most people want to make a lot of money, get that job, go to that college, and get that degree as they believe that to be their purpose. However, just because you go to that college, get that degree, and lock in that highly-paying job doesn't mean you are on the correct path that destiny has chosen.

There are millions of people with the highest-paying jobs, and they still find themselves with bouts of depression. Depression is a major sign that you are on the wrong path, you are not following your destiny, and you are drifting away from your purpose in life. Ignoring signs so conspicuous will push you farther down into the quicksand, making it nearly impossible for you to get out of it.

My turning point was when I had an event happen to me around the age of 16, after which I completely shifted. I started experimenting more with my own mindset, spirituality, and mental attitude. It was one of those instances when your sixth sense tells you whether you should do it or not. My sixth sense told me to take care of my mindset, spirituality, and mental attitude, and I listened to it.

I started to listen more to the inner voice, and the more I became self-aware, I found myself taking a different path than I normally would. It seemed like the energy inside me was on a positive note. I started to feel the black hole that seemed to envelop my heart and make everything cold inside me eating away, and it started disappearing like it was never there.

It seems like the farther you get down in the black hole, the harder it is to get out. It happens when you get farther away from your goal or true destiny, what you are supposed to do with your life, or what really gives you happiness and joy. This black hole that we call depression keeps growing. I have been there just like billions of other people, but I have also gotten out of it. I hope you, too, get to do that once you are done with this book.

You can be the richest person in the world, with the prettiest girl or the handsome guy, but if you are not on the road to your true destiny, that hole inside you will grow bigger and bigger.

I noticed that when I got on the right path and followed my heart, my dreams, and what I was supposed to do in life, that hole got smaller and smaller. I could see the light at the end of this long tunnel of depression that I had been trying to get out of. I started to feel energized because I had finally found my purpose in life. So, all my life experiences, experiments, and beliefs have led me to write this book that I feel is the memoir of life, not just my life but everyone's life. Thus, I hope this book opens up everyone's mind in a way that will help them get on the right path and do what they should do to feel productive and not lost. In a way that will help them start living their life in hopes that it will make sense. In a way that will help them to discover who they are and where they're going. Sit back and relax. Hopefully, you will enjoy this book, as I have tried to write it using simple vocabulary so that everyone can understand it and enjoy it.

Contents

Introduction

My name is Victor Dyastinteen, and I was born into an American family. I was like any other American boy, but I had the gift of foresight. They say the less you know, the better. I disagree because, as a kid, I was always looking for answers to everything unknown to me.

I had a keen interest in astronomy and space exploration, basically anything that was related to science or anything that science dealt with.

Robots and computers appealed to me, but my fascination didn't just stop there. I had to know how things worked. I needed to know how we get a picture using radio- waves that give color to the image. I could just not see things how they appeared; I had to always take things apart to see how they worked and then put them back together again.

However, I never performed well in school and never got high grades or anything of the sort until I was in junior high school, which is where I excelled in science and mathematics. I was always good with my hands and would build things out of metals and wood, but I was still just an average young American boy.

I was born a Catholic and was baptized to follow my father's religion. I had to go to Catechism to study about Jesus and the Virgin Mary. There, I got to learn the prayers of our Father and Hail Mary, the 'Apostles' creed, and more. Religion has always been a large part of my life because of my religious upbringing. I have always been that person who believes in God the Almighty and has faith that there is something beyond this life. I believe in

The Creator because how could it be possible otherwise that among all of the billions of galaxies, there is our planet that is at the right distance away from the sun and has the possibility to sustain life out of all the other planets? However, I do not only believe in life on Earth, which is carbon-based lifeforms, but life, nonetheless. It could be a methane-based life form, which is not life as we know it but life above and beyond our thinking.

I believe that if you can conceive something in your mind, then you should have the ability to create what you have conceived.

The supernatural always intrigued me as a kid, and even now, especially the Unknown. Even as a kid, I started to wonder about the human body or mind and what it can do.

However, as I grew older, I started to meditate to see if I could invoke change within my body by using my mind. I realized that when I closed my eyes real tight, I could see various shapes and images in various shades of gray and white. So, I started to concentrate on those shapes and suddenly realized that those shapes started to form images, like trees, rocks, buildings, and other familiar things. Sometimes, when I meditated deeply, I felt myself getting ready to fall asleep due to meditation. Right at that moment, when a person is neither awake nor asleep, lies the boundary where the mind is freed.

There, the mind is free to roam wherever it likes. At that moment, sometimes I saw people as if I was floating above them or right in front of them, but it was as if they could not see me. Sometimes, the people were walking around or were in an area like a mall or a park.

Most people call this Astro-projection, where your essence or your soul actually leaves your body and travels to other places. I found this concept very interesting, which led me to practice Astro-projection even more. In practicing it, I used to fly like a jet, skimming across the water or the hills and through the forest down to the city, watching people as they do their business. I became so fascinated with astral projection that I wondered if it is only confined to Earth or if one can go beyond that. The next time I tried astral projection, I set my sights high, really high. I soared up through the sky, through the clouds, and zoomed past the moon, past Mars, and on to Jupiter. It was unlike anything I had ever experienced before and only took a matter of seconds.

At this point, I doubted myself and looked back to see if I could see Mother Earth. Lo and behold, I saw what everyone had always talked about: the silver thread that attaches our Astro-projecting body in the astral world with our real body back home. In that instant of doubt, I felt myself being yanked back in a matter of seconds; it was fascinating.

Then, I went on to practice deep meditation, which I decided to call "mind syncing." It was like a journey, unlike anything I had ever done. It calmed and gave me focus and peace of mind. It happens when you sync your mind, body, and soul. One day, when I was "mind syncing," I laid my head on my pillow and closed my eyes. When I started to mind sync, I could see past my eyelids and then through the ceiling.

Not just that, I then saw the beautiful stars as they were spread across the sky. At some distance, I saw something like some kind of light very faintly, but it appeared to be approaching me. As I gazed upon this light, I noticed that it was forming a cylinder of rectangular sections of light with various lengths.

As it drew closer, the pattern started becoming very distinct; it even appeared to be rotating around its center. I was mesmerized by this white pattern of light; it was like nothing I had seen before. I was so lost in admiring it, not knowing that it was getting closer and closer to the point where it hit me in the forehead. It felt like I had just been electrocuted, and I saw sparks flying here and there while my whole body was shaking and convulsing.

I opened my eyes, wondering if I had fallen asleep and hoping that everything that had just transpired had been a dream. As I came back to my senses, I found every inch of my body aching and in cold sweat. I still don't know to this day if it really happened or if I was dreaming. All I know is that my life has never been the same from that day forward.

Nowadays, I find myself looking at things to see how they work, but I can also see how they can be made to work even better. I have started to become interested in radiation, nuclear physics, engineering, and even mathematics. Several years after that night, a light came on, and suddenly, I became aware of my life purpose and what I needed to do to achieve that goal. From that day onward, I started seeing life in a new light. I embraced my intuition so that it could lead me to my destiny. Now, I don't expect all of you to believe in what I experienced but only to read this book and take something from it, which can give you the knowledge to help you succeed in becoming the real you.

Chapter 1: Science

To begin, we will need an introduction to science because science has a relationship with everything in the world and the Universe, whether it is light, energy, matter, antimatter, or emotions. Science is the key to everything because it binds us all together and intertwines everything that is and that will ever be.

You must realize that all matter in the Universe, including all of the planets, stars, and chemicals, has always existed. You cannot create matter, and the same is true for energy. All of the energy required to bind all of the atoms together to make all of the molecules have always been present since the beginning of time and will always be present because of the one thing about science: the laws of conservation of energy and conservation of matter, which are two key concepts that have been proven by today's scientists, and will be explained later in the book. Let's start with frequency. A displacement of time over distance and the amplitudes between these peaks and valleys are referred to as wavelengths. Science has already demonstrated that frequencies can have both constructive and destructive interference.

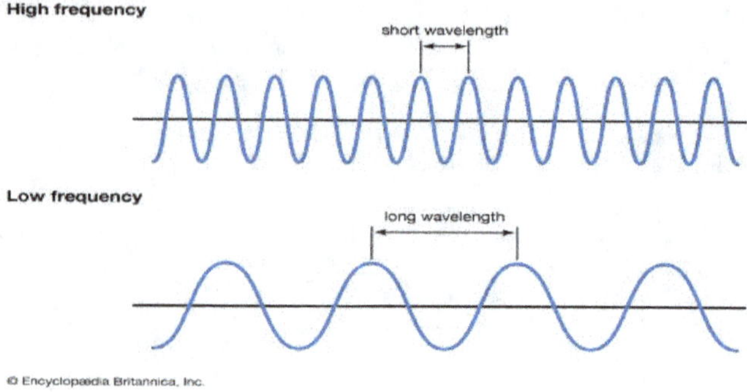

Constructive harmonic interaction occurs when two frequencies with the same amplitude come together and have the same height of the peaks and valleys within a certain time frame. This results in harmonic interaction, which combines both frequencies into one with an increase in amplitude, 1+1= 2, corresponding to an increase in power output, known as energy conservation.

Now, you can have other wavelengths of frequency/energy that oppose each other so that when they come together, the portion of the frequency that is similar but opposite of each other will cancel each other out, leaving the remainder behind and, in some cases, wholly canceled out, which is known as destructive interaction, this is how your noise canceling headphone work to eliminate unwanted sounds.

On the other hand, frequencies are waves, like our human DNA, that can store information, so each point of a wave can be the source of a new wave. For example, you can send sound energy toward a barrier or a wall. If there is a hole in that barrier, it will generate a new wave on the other side, which will begin to spread out as if it were the original wave that started the whole process due to the conservation of energy.

Now Matter.

What is it?

In the world of science, everything in the Universe is essentially made up of two key components: matter and energy. Matter consists of tiny particles known as electrons, neutrons, and protons, which are held together by energy. When these particles are arranged in a specific way, substances are created.

These substances can vary widely, from water to metals to the air we breathe, the planets, the stars, and all the chemicals that have always been here. It all depends on how the electrons, neutrons, and protons are arranged.

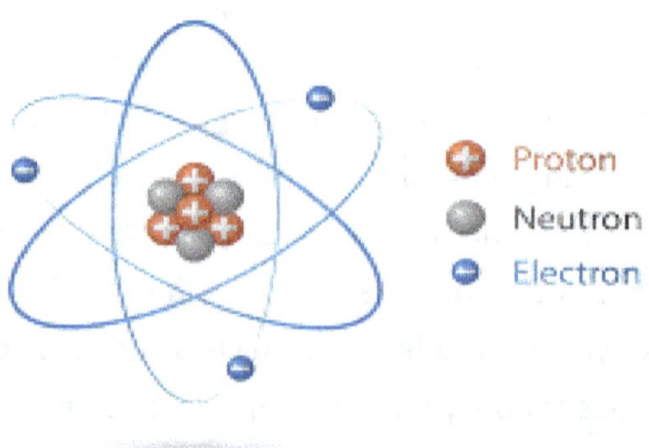

Matter has existed since the beginning of time and cannot be created or destroyed; it can only be transformed from one state to another. It can be turned from a solid to a liquid to a gaseous state, and if you recall that we are all made up of matter and that the energy that links the Universe together is the same energy that bonds us together, this will lead us to another subject: what are souls made of.

We all start out as matter when we are born with 23 chromosomes from the mother and 23 chromosomes from the father, but it's something more than just genes at play. The transfer of energy from our parents allows us to be our own beings. The energy has a special way of storing information, such as memories, which we can use later in life. These memories are stored in bio-electrical signals in our brain, and it is these memories that give rise to our soul. If we were to clone a person, the clone might have many of the original person's traits, thoughts, and feelings because they share a lot of the same characteristics. It's almost like the information is passed along.

Take a baby snake just born, for example. It somehow knows what to do to survive even though it's never been taught. This knowledge is stored because the energy that gives the snake life carries the survival traits of its mother. It doesn't need years of teaching; it's born with this instinct.

For more complex beings like us, learning and understanding things takes longer because we have more going on in our lives and minds. So, we need time to become adept at handling the complexities of life.

Science has shown that there's a mathematical equation to figure out how much energy is needed to bind all those particles together in matter. Moreover, matter cannot exist without energy and vice versa, so they share a symbiotic relationship. This concept is just like music. Just as the right notes create music played at different frequencies, which are vibrational energies, in science, energies bind molecules together and form matter. When these energies are balanced and harmonious, a stable structure is achieved like a regular piece of steel. However, when the structure is unstable, there's still a kind of harmonic interaction, but it's destructive. The energies no longer align correctly, leading to destructive forces. This instability can result in the release of radiation or thermal energy.

Constructive harmonic interactions, on the other hand, are like the way different notes in music come together. When they harmonize, it creates a pleasant and positive experience, just like your favorite song. Even if you didn't initially like a tune, if its frequencies resonate with you, you might grow to enjoy it over time.

As I mentioned, when things clash, like notes in an inharmonious melody, it becomes destructive interference, leading to negative reactions. It's like being near someone whose energy doesn't match yours, resulting in discomfort and your guard going up.

Harmonic interactions occur all around us. It's not just in music; it's in how light lets us see the world. Light carries specific frequencies that determine colors and what we perceive. When someone's energy frequency aligns with yours, you might find them attractive, like a beautiful sight.

It's just like driving with your favorite song on; you might not notice you're going faster, but it's a positive interaction that affects your state of being. This relationship extends to even the simplest aspects of our lives, like our emotions- happiness, sadness, love, and even inexplicable feelings toward others. Another way to illustrate this is by thinking of frequency as one complete cycle, going up one foot (positive) and then down one foot (negative) over a certain period of time. This is one cycle.

Now, if you have five cycles per minute, repeat these one-foot loops five times in one minute. So, for each cycle, imagine it carries one cup of water. With constructive interference, these cups add up, and at the end of one minute, you'd have five cups of water because everything lines up nicely.

On the other hand, with destructive interference, because the frequency isn't perfectly balanced on both sides, it's like losing part or all of that cup of water at the end of each cycle. So, instead of having more cups, you might end up with none because things aren't aligning. Let's simplify all of this with some relatable examples. One example is a blind date, which is like a science experiment in a way. Whether it turns out great or not so great depends on how well you and your date "click."

If there's too much "destructive interference,' 'meaning you both clash and it's all negative, well, chances are neither of you will want a second date, like mixing oil and water, which just won't blend no matter how hard you try. They don't harmonize; they repel each other.

But, if you're on a date, and everything feels right, it's like a beautiful harmony in a song. Your frequencies match, and you have a great time. The conversation flows, and it's all positive, like mixing two very similar liquids. They blend effortlessly, and you have a perfect blend, just like water, and a flavor that matches.

It's all about the harmonic interactions we have with our surroundings, whether they enhance our experiences (constructive) or diminish them (destructive). This concept can help people understand why they have good or bad days and feel various emotions in different situations.

Wave Interference

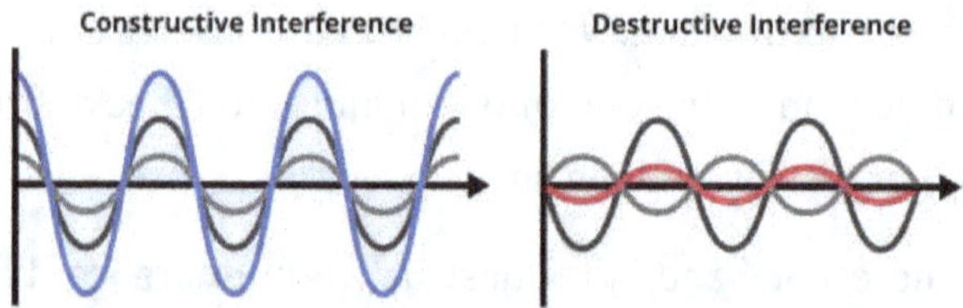

At the core of it, we're all composed of energy and matter, each with our individual body frequency that influences how we interact positively or negatively with the world around us. This way of looking at science makes it more accessible and relatable, as it's easy to get lost in complex numbers and symbols, which can feel like a different language to many. And it is, but only a few can understand that language.

Similarly, understanding the basics of matter and energy is like finding the key to unlock a vast world of knowledge.

From there, you can explore all sorts of things, from how blind dates work to why oil and water won't mix.

Therefore, everything needs balance to work. Science can calculate things precisely, just like figuring out how many atoms are in a molecule of uranium. Things work smoothly when they are balanced, like in a harmonious song or in nature. But you have chaos when they're not, like on a bad date or a mix of oil and water. The goal is to help you grasp this big picture, understand where they fit in, and how to have better life interactions, whether positive or negative. So, that's why sharing this knowledge is incredibly important. It helps us understand why things happen and how we can make our lives better and more peaceful.

Chapter 2: The Universe

When we talk about the beginning, we talk about how life began on Earth, evolved from water animals to land animals, transitioned from monkeys to humans, and all those things. What if the Creator created Amy and Eve not to be lovers but to be companions, only with A-sexual gender.

Much like some frogs that are A-sexual and don't need a mate to procreate, and when the time is right, they produce offspring. This seems to be more probable because it minimizes incest in order to build the population of humankind.

However, how life began is still a mystery; it is believed that a lot happened before that. Organic life began approximately 3.7 billion years ago, but cosmic life started 13.7 billion years ago when the Universe was formed.

The Universe is the first thing that came into being; everything followed after it. There are a thousand explanations for how the Universe was formed.

All seemed hard to believe at first, but then Albert Einstein gave his theory of relativity, which stated that space and time are relative. It basically established that the laws of physics are the same everywhere, making the Big Bang theory the most plausible explanation for how the Universe was formed.

It began as a vast vacuum of space, where a single massive sphere of matter existed at the center of the universe.

Since space is a void of any known matter and or elements, we shall call it Antimatter. The Antimatter and the sphere of matter were the only two things present at the beginning. Not even time existed back then, just matter and its counterpart, antimatter.

We now know that matter wants to be in a state of balance at all times. When things become unbalanced, chaos ensues, and something extremely violent can be created. For reasons unknown, the balance between matter and Antimatter changed, causing a cataclysmic event, creating an explosion so massive that a hot and dense environment was created, where energy manifested itself.

It led to the creation of electrons, neutrons, protons, and some other small particles that exist within matter. This sphere of matter expanded; it was like a molten hot ball. This fight between matter and antimatter was the main event that was the creation of time.

The reaction between matter and antimatter started multiplying itself; it contained so much energy that its high temperature resulted in an explosion. The matter got scattered through the Cosmos. The blast was so impactful that it punctured a hole through space and time and is now called The Big Bang. The Big Bang Theory is an incredible enlightenment of how everything began. The explosion was the event that created time and cast out all of the matter that was, is, and will be into the vacuum of space.

Before this, time didn't exist because no such event or activity had occurred to create a starting point so that one could get to the end. It was nothingness before 'time' came into existence.

Do you know what a sound barrier is? The sound barrier is an invisible wall.

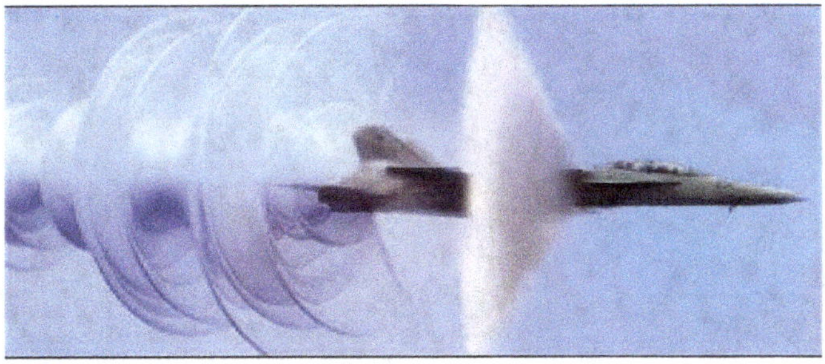

When something approaches the speed of sound, that wall starts to deform in the direction of the traveling object, and if that object exceeds the speed of sound, it deforms that wall and punctures a hole in the sound barrier, creating a sonic boom.

The Big Bang is an explanation of how that explosion ripped a hole through space and time because it also has a wall like the sound barrier, and there are consequences if it is broken. This explosion could be converted to a frequency that has a positive amplitude (explosion) followed by a negative amplitude (implosion).

The Big Bang theory which describes how the positive explosion that cast out all the matter in the cosmos to help create galaxies, nebulas, and planets also punctured a hole through the space/time continuum, which led to the creation of gravity. The event caused massive disruption, but nature wants everything in balance, so to counteract this positive explosion force, nature introduced a negative force called implosion to help close the hole in the space/time continuum, and due to no friction in the vacuum, it created a pulsating hole. This phenomenon is called spatial incursion, also known as gravity.

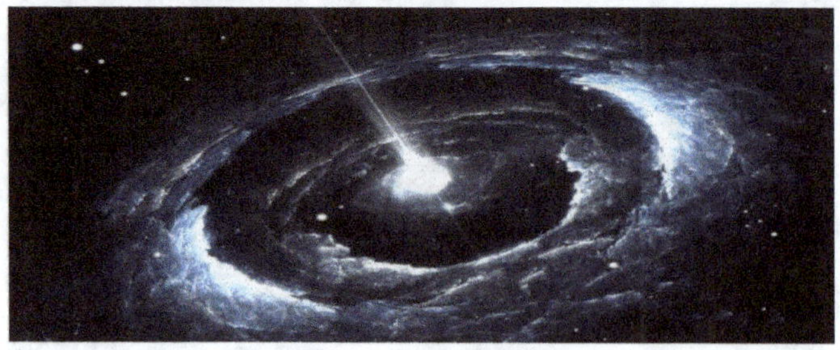

Gravity didn't exist before this spatial incursion because there was no need for it; it came into existence to pull all the matter back toward its center. Force, i.e., gravity, was created to bring balance back to the cosmos. The problem with matter moving in space is that there is no resistance or friction to slow it down. The absence of friction in space leads to a continuous motion and or oscillation between positive (Explosion) and negative (Implosion) forces.

It is said that if something is moving in space at a certain speed or a certain velocity, it will keep on moving at that speed and velocity until it comes in contact with something equal or opposite to its force to neutralize it, which we know today as "Newton's 1st Law of Motion."

This spatial incursion of the positive explosion in the positive side of the space/time barrier and the negative implosion to bring everything to a balance and close this hole, this dance between explosion/implosion of the space/time barrier resulted in the creation of gravity, a force that nature engineered to claim the massive explosion and to bring all matter back to its true center. When matter was expelled into the cosmos as a result of the Big Bang, nature created gravity to repair the damage caused by the Big Bang, and when matter of any size comes in contact with gravity, which is energy/frequency that will go through a metamorphosis called Inductive Reactance, which will generate its own gravitational waves through this process.

The phenomenon of inductive reactance is a basic scientific fact that if you pass a wire through a magnetic field, it will generate an electric current through that wire. The same is true with gravity since it can act like a wave and or frequency. When gravity comes in contact with matter through inductive reactance, that matter generates a secondary gravity wave that is proportionate to its density, massive density, then you will get a massive gravitational attraction, and microscopic density will produce a microscopic attraction. The Big Bang, which cast out all the matter into the depth of space, expanded from the central point in the Universe outward. Astronomers call this a red shift when everything moves outward, away from its original center (Expansion).

Astronomers state that at some point, gravity will slow down and stop the expansion of matter, and because nature wants everything to be in balance, gravity will correct what the Big Bang started. Thus, the blue shift represents a mass (Contraction) event that will eventually return the matter toward the center from where it came, driven by gravity. Current physicists say that the core of a planet creates gravity, but what about planets with no molten core or a large asteroid that might be hollow?

Before planets were formed, they didn't have gravity during the Big Bang because they were just large chunks of hot molten rocks and dust with no core. When our solar system was formed, and gravity started to interact with everything, then everything should have just stayed where it was. There was no reason for it to be pulled back to the original center and go through the period called the blue shift. This is where my concept of gravity differs from others.

Astro-physicists say that gravity is generated within each planet and interacts with all the other planets in the Universe.

This doesn't make a lot of sense to me because if that is the case, then all celestial bodies would stay where they are, and there would not have to be a blue shift. If every planet had its own gravity, everything would be chaotic, and the planets would get attracted to each other while continuing a redshift (Expansion). There would be no center position to be pulled back to.

But then again, gravity is a frequency/energy which can have a positive and a negative amplitude. My theory is we know that when a wave/frequency is generated, any point of the original primary gravity wave known as (PG1) can be a source of a new wave. As the PG1 wave propagates outward, when it comes in contact with matter, that matter becomes the source of a new wave/gravity called secondary gravity wave (SG1), and so on. This process is called inductive reactance.

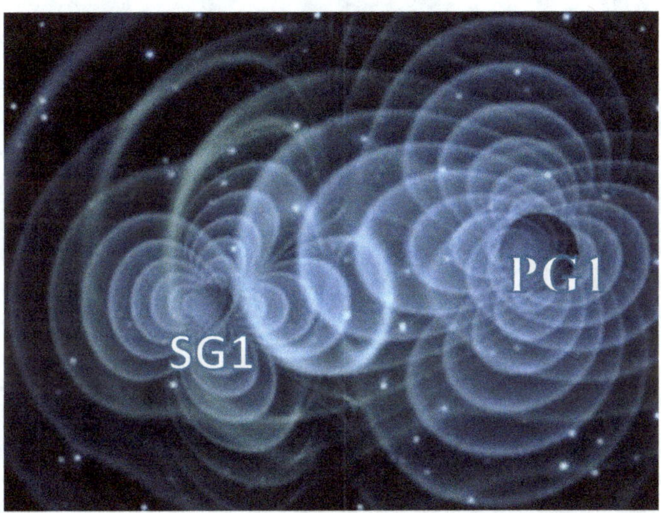

Now, gravity works the same way when it comes to inductive reactance, as when the gravity/wave hits a planet, that planet becomes a new point of that gravity/wave, and that planet can now generate its own gravity in proportion to its density, the higher the density of that matter, the stronger the gravity wave it will generate that will travel outward from this new position. This phenomenon is true for all the billions and trillions of chunks of matter that are out there.

For example, the primary gravity wave (PG1) travels outward from its original center, and as it comes in contact with matter, it generates a secondary gravity wave SG1, then SG2, then SG3, and so on until all the trillions of pieces of matter go through the same process creating trillions of SG waves. Now, remember what we discussed in the previous chapters? What happens when we have a positive and a negative energy/frequency coming in contact with each other?

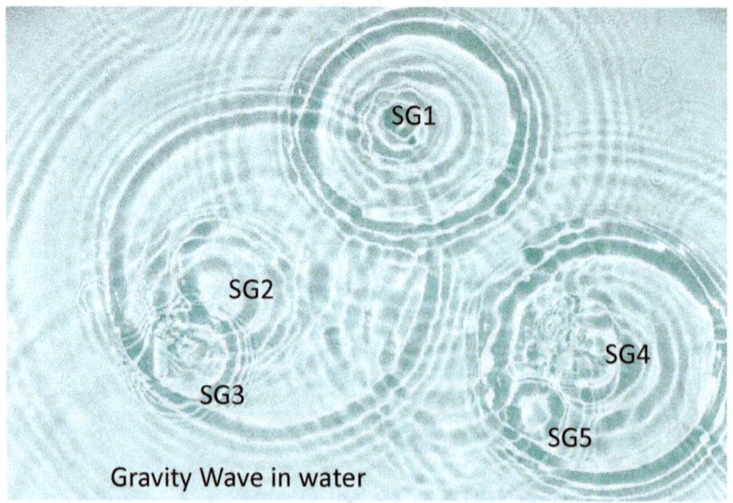

Gravity Wave in water

If the two forces in question are equal and opposite from each other, they cancel each other out, while others that match will increase in amplitude. If you were to make a map showing all the matter, big or small, that had been cast outward from the center of the cosmos. First, draw a small circle at the original center to represent the PG1 wave; keep making more circles with a slightly bigger distance between them, creating rings around the PG1 wave traveling outward. These rings will keep getting bigger and further away from their original center for eternity, but when they come in contact with matter, that matter will generate its own gravitational wave, SG1, and will continue moving outward from this new original center for eternity.

Now, draw small circles that represent the positive/negative gravity waves around SG1 the same as you did with PG1, and increase the distance of both the PG1 and SG1 as they move outward from their original center. Do the same when either of the gravity waves hits other pieces of matter and so on until every particle of matter has its own rings representing the gravity wave.

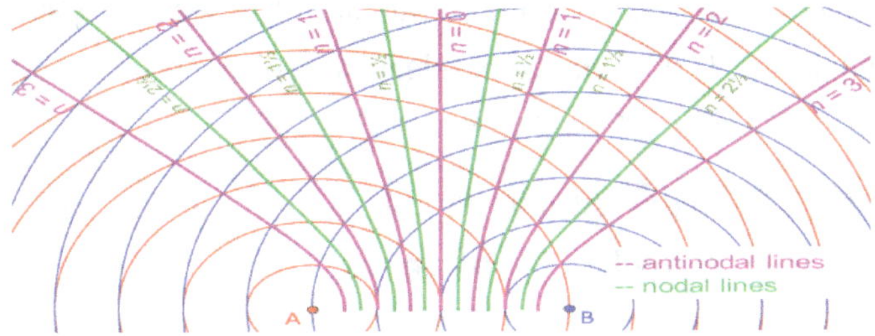

Every time the lines of a gravitational wave intersect or touch another gravity wave's rings, at that point of contact, they cancel out a percentage of the wave.

As they intersect, the trillions of gravity lines, which we will call these fringe lines, will cancel out even more of that secondary gravity wave (SG). This is why there is not 100% gravity attraction pulling the chunks of matter back to the center. It might start at 1% attractive force because the other 99% was canceled out by destructive interaction of the secondary gravity wave, and with every cycle it goes through, more and more of the fringe gravitational wave is canceled out by the secondary gravity fringe lines. At some point, perhaps a trillion more years down the road, as this process keeps happening, the attractive force will increase to 4% and then 8%, and so on, until all of the secondary gravity waves (SG) will get canceled out, leaving only the primary gravity waves (PG1) with 100% attractive force.

That's when the redshift will stop, and we will truly begin the blue shift. That's when everything can be pulled back to its original center. Everything coming back to its original center will result in another explosion, AKA Big Bang. The question that comes to mind is, how many Big Bangs have there been? Is this our first one? What if it's our 100th, or even one-billionth?

None of us really knows where we are, except for the timeline we are experiencing right now. Pondering over the science of the Universe, I have concluded that it's perhaps nature's way of recycling everything, starting fresh. With the next Big Bang, our Universe will end, and perhaps a new one will begin.

Chapter 3: Spirituality

Spirituality encompasses a profound understanding of our existence; it connects the divine, be it Almighty, Allah, Yahweh, Shaddai, or from this point forward, shall be known as The Creator of the universe. The Creator is the alpha and omega of all existence. Our Creator is the supreme being who is both the origin and the culmination of all existence. They say that the Creator knows everything that has happened and will happen. They say that the Creator knows everything one thinks, what one needs, and what goes on in one's heart. Everything from an apple falling from its tree to a plane taking off from New York airport — all is known to the Creator before it happens.

They say the Creator knows what you will be doing ten years from now on a Monday at 3 PM in the afternoon. Some might call this blind faith or predestination, but with many roads that can change with every decision you make, it is still all science. Everything I just stated isn't something I made up myself; it is probably as real as your existence or even more. The Creator being, the alpha and omega of all existence, symbolizes the eternal and infinite nature of spirituality. Spirituality is subjective in nature, but if one looks at the science behind it, then it can be said that it's not singular.

The existence of humans can be characterized into two distinct categories. One is the physical existence of the body, and then there is an energy that keeps us breathing and allows for conscience, faith, and or spiritual existence. Our soul is our spiritual existence, which was put inside this matter, a body made of various compounds.

Our spiritual existence, the soul that has a symbiotic relationship inside this body of flesh and bone (Matter), our existence, is just life experienced at a point in time that has been stored in our brain as a bio-electric frequency, which has a specific energy.

The energy that binds the universe together is the same energy that binds humans, birds, bees, flowers, and trees together. It can be measured and is called the Bio-Ethereal frequency (BEF) as such because it itself has matter and energy.

The ability of energy to have constructive and destructive interactions is what forms the relationship between humans, our planet, and the cosmos. The relationship between all matter is solely a culmination of different body frequencies of matter consisting of all types of compounds.

On the other hand, we can't prove that the Creator does not exist as any form of matter. Therefore, no one can say that the Creator is a man or a woman. The Creator is simply an omnipotent intelligent energy that knows what needs to be done to maintain a balance in nature and matter.

Everything in nature needs to have balance. Imbalance brings chaos and just a slew of other things that come with it. In terms of spirituality, if the Creator is an all-knowing energy, then we, as people, with all of our life experiences that get stored in our brains in the form of energy, have a connection with The Creator. By saying that all of our dreams, hopes, emotions, and life experiences exist in the form of energy, we are attesting to the fact that the Almighty knows everything.

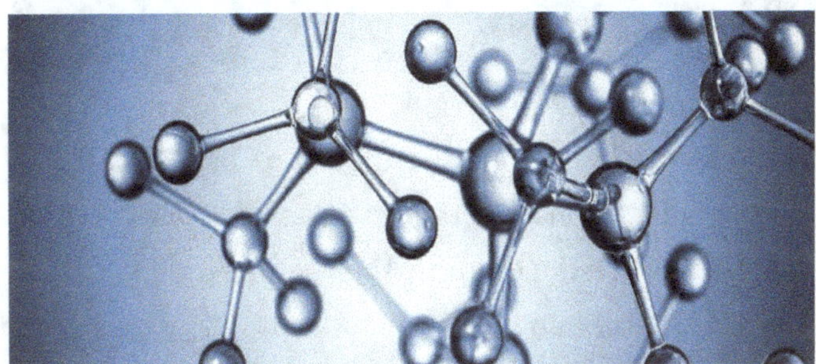

The molecules and compounds we are made of are bound together by the energy that The Creator is made of, the omnipotent energy. Therefore, it can be said that we all share the same energy as The Creator. This reveals that every part of us that is made out of matter will deteriorate and go back into the earth to blend with the other matter. However, the energy part of us, which is our soul, our memories, and our emotions, all stored electrically inside the matter we call our brain, will exist forever.

Once the body or matter is gone, the energy that was stored in-the brain electrically can't be destroyed; it can only be released and converted or recycled.

At death, everything that makes us up, all the billions of memories, are just points in time or moments that we experience with our loved ones, family, and friends. All the happy or sad emotions that we feel and all the adventures that we have are cast out into the cosmos at great speed.

Remember that the energy that gave us life is the same energy that binds atoms together to make molecules that are the building blocks of all the cosmos. They get recycled, and they get absorbed into something in order to keep this wonderful thing that we call life going. Moreover, since the Creator is this all-knowing energy, at death, all that energy that's cast out into the cosmos actually goes back to the Creator. Now we know how it's possible for the Creator to know everything that is, has ever been, and will ever be.

Please let me clarify this chapter so that you can understand how spirituality connects all matter and all living things together. Now, as the matter that forms us is held together by energy, the same energy that our thoughts and emotions that are being stored electrically in our brains are part of the same energy.

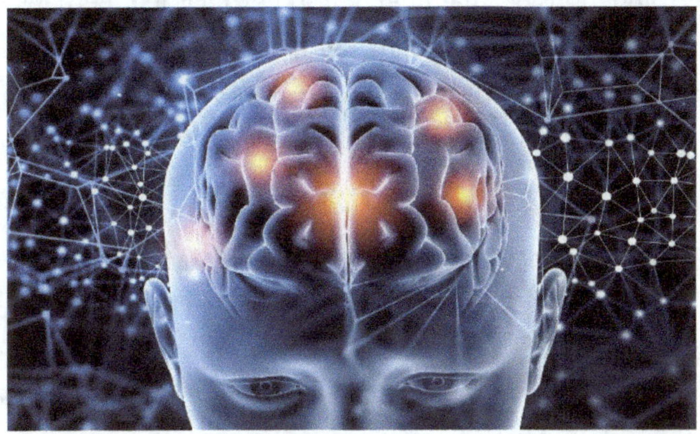

Since energy cannot be destroyed, it can be converted so that it can be used in other ways. As a result, the energy that was us gets to live on forever.

At death, this energy gets intertwined with everything else in the galaxy. It can either become part of a water molecule or the atomic structure of a tree. It can either get absorbed in the vacuum of space itself or become part of Saturn's ring.

We don't know where, just that when duty calls, you respond, but the best part is that your memories are going to live on for eternity, where the Creator can have access to our thoughts, dreams, emotions, and our entire existence in the blink of an eye.

The Creator becomes us, knows us, knows all life that was, is, and will be because the energy that is us gets recycled like all of the other things that exist in nature. Since our emotions, feelings, and experiences are information that gets stored biochemically in our body when energy is recycled, a person's qualities that were trapped inside that energy also get recycled. Perhaps it is possible that when a person is born, somehow the barrier that separates the information that was stored in an energy might bleed out.

Consequently, when you look at remarkable people, for instance, a musical composer of your time who is only a teenager but whose music is Beethoven-level great even though he has never heard Beethoven's music in his life, it's probably because some of the energy which that person is utilizing belongs to Beethoven in another space-time continuum.

In this context, one could say that the DNA stored in an energy that belongs to you in a past life can be brought to the surface in another person's present life.

If such is the case, information can be exchanged without the long process of learning to obtain such knowledge, which can help promote a society to go further.

This explains why we get Deja vu, the feeling that this has happened before. It's not just you; maybe it's another person who experienced that same situation. The boundary between your life and the energy that makes us up drifted over into your current state of consciousness.

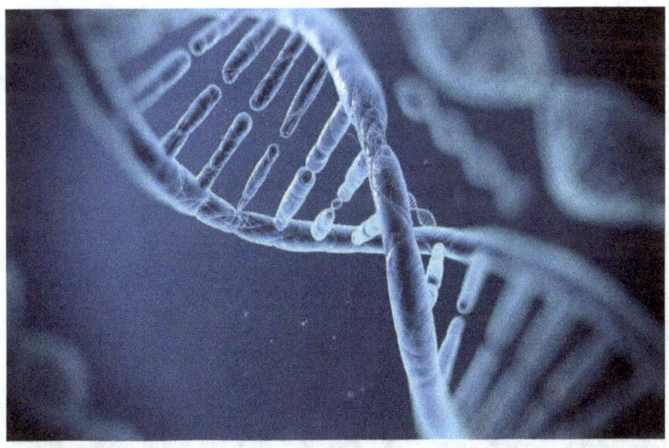

This is just a probability, but if this perhaps happens, it helps explain what nature is doing in the background in everyday life. It also tells us that we need to evolve. If we as a society don't evolve, then we will become stagnant. Usually, after that stagnation comes death. In this way, life is much like water. If water is constantly running through a stream, it can form or sustain life. However, if you stop that stream from moving, water can become stagnant. The stagnant water then turns into a breeding ground for diseases, and if you drink from that water, it can kill you. Thus, the water can give you life and can also take it away. To avoid stagnation, we as a society must keep moving, i.e., growing and evolving. Now, we have to use our imagination when we think about life, not the life that we know of here on Earth, but life on other planets has to be taken into account. There are millions of galaxies that astronomers have calculated to be in existence today, and all of those galaxies have a sun. In the solar system, if a planet is at the right distance from the sun, it is possible to have humanoid life (carbon-based life forms). Now, since we have hundreds of chemicals on our periodic table, so there is a probability that silicon-based life forms, methane-based life forms, or even oxygen-based life forms may be able to exist at other distances closer to and or farther from the sun.

So, when we talk about spirituality, we must include all life forms here on Earth and other planets. Let's use Star Trek as an example to outline possible societies other than our own. The Klingons are a warrior race of life forms; war governs their society.

The Vulcans are ruled by logic, and you may have other civilizations that are ruled by their emotions, art, and even music. If all of these various types of civilizations do not evolve or change to accommodate future conditions, then they can perish, and that civilization would cease to exist. The best example would be the warrior race. If they do not embrace logic, then eventually, their society will succumb to constant war, which will end in their demise. Similarly, other examples can be viewed of all the other societies, and it can be said that if they don't embrace little of everything to become a balanced society, they will perish too.

By utilizing the same beliefs of the Creator as we did with the human race here on earth and utilize that same situation for all of the other worlds throughout the cosmos with the recycling of souls because we are all made of matter and energy, and all energy has a frequency that can have destructive or constructive interaction with all energies and or matter. Therefore, through the recycling of souls, the transfer of knowledge from other civilizations and or from other worlds is highly probable.

Now, you start to see the similarities of what we all share with everything in the cosmos. The one key commonality is frequency, i.e., energy. Without it, we wouldn't exist. Without frequencies, we wouldn't have gravity. The regulation of those frequencies is what helps a civilization to evolve. Without evolution, there will be death.

Thus, to not die out as a society, we must keep evolving. We have to look at where we are now and think about where we need to be 100 or 300 years from now. If we don't evolve to accommodate the changes that will occur, then, like all other great societies that came before us, we will fall as well.

Chapter 4: Relationships

Finding the right partner in today's world is like navigating a maze – seemingly easy, yet strangely complex. Relationships are no walk in the park; they're not just about spotting someone cute and deciding to give it a shot. They can be very delicate, and if you don't pay attention, you might find yourself in a breakup loop.

Many blame it on the complexity of the modern world, but let's dig a little deeper. Relationships aren't fragile because of the chaos in the external world; their volatility comes from the inner workings of humans.

This is because everything around us, including our bodies, hums with specific frequencies. So, when it comes to relationships, think of them as a cosmic dance between two entities made up of matter and energy, each with its own unique frequency.

Now, these frequencies aren't just vibes; they can actually collide like waves in a pond; they start out as small ripples, then small waves, which can turn into a tsunami due to constructive interference. It's a bit like when sound waves sync up beautifully (constructive interference), creating musical harmony. But, on the flip side, if these frequencies clash destructively, it's like a cosmic breakup button – slowly eroding the connection between two individuals until it fizzles out.

So, imagine this: everyone carries around their own unique vibe, a personal frequency I like to call the bio-ethereal frequency (B.E.F). It's like your cosmic signature, as distinct as a fingerprint – no duplicates.

Now, here's the fascinating part. These individual frequencies or (B.E.F.)? They're not just random signals. They set the stage for a kind of harmonic symphony when people interact. Ever met someone and felt an instant connection, as if you've known them forever? That's your bio-ethereal frequency dancing in tune with theirs.

Call it science fiction, but in reality, it's science fact! Just like scientists can analyze the composition of substances on faraway planets by studying their frequencies, we, in a way, pick up on the bio-ethereal frequency or vibes people project. That person who catches your eye?

It's almost as if they're beaming a unique light that resonates with your wavelength/B.E.F., creating that magnetic pull. Love at first sight? It's as simple as a cosmic frequency match.

Picture this: A beam of light is really made up of multiple frequencies, and when light bounces off someone or something, whatever frequencies that someone or something is made of get soaked in or absorbed, and the rest bounces off and is what we see, or rather what we don't see. Remember, everything wants to be in balance, but since a part of the light gets absorbed, it is that missing spectrum of light that our mind can see, so we crave it in order to complete the picture; they're the ones that paint the picture – what you see. So, when you say you're falling for someone, it's not necessarily the whole person but more like the visual energy they're throwing your way.

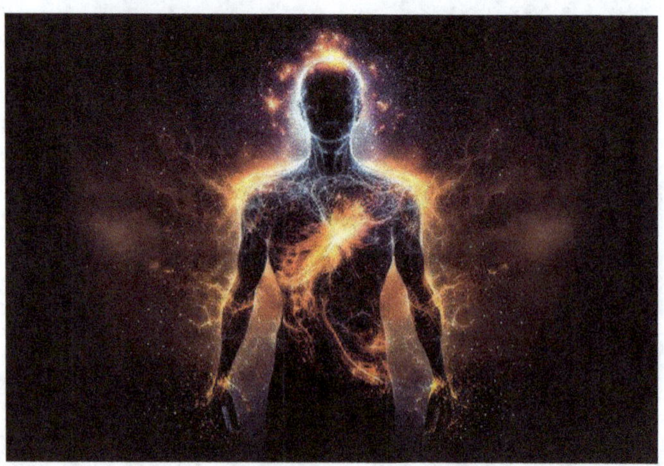

Now, here's the kicker. It's this metaphysical vibe or connection, and you can't tweak it. Sure, you can be smitten by their looks, but that's just one-tenth piece of the puzzle. Your ideal partner, your soulmate, they're more than just a pretty face. It's about those unseen aspects, the stuff that decides whether your connection is a flash in the pan or a lasting saga.

Will your love withstand the sands of time, going strong after fifty years, or is it a fleeting spark that burns out in a day, a month, or a year? That's where the real magic lies.

Ever heard of a relationship matrix? It's a cosmic cheat code to figure out if someone's your ideal match. This matrix is a ten-part masterpiece; each section can be 100 positive and or negative points that can total up to a thousand possible points, positive and or negative per person, leaving a possible 2000 positive and or negative scores as a couple. The higher your potential combined scores, the better your shot at a forever kind of love. So, before you dive into the deep end of love at first sight, this matrix can be your crystal ball.

Based on this, let's dissect the whole love at first sight thing. It's like a visual attraction, right? If it feels like a magical spell, that's a constructive interaction – the kind that makes you say, "I fell in love at first sight."

But imagine if it was the opposite, a destructive vibe – you'd probably dislike them on the spot for no apparent reason. It's all in the metaphysical frequencies, the cosmic chemistry. No matter how hard you try, you can't rewrite the script of what you feel. It's the universe playing matchmaker, giving you a cosmic hint on who you should choose.

When your cosmic frequency, also known as Bio-Ethereal Frequency, collides with another, it creates a combination that can have three possible outcomes: positive, negative, or somewhere in between (neutral). This cosmic tango determines whether that person is truly your soulmate. Visual attraction is just the tip of the iceberg; there's also the sound, smell, touch, taste, sex, intellect, activities, personality, and bio-ethereal frequency – all forging this emotional connection that tightly binds two souls until death becomes the parting force.

So, you might fall head over heels at first glance, but the next part of the matrix tells the truth. It's the audible side of things – the voice, the sound, the symphony of frequencies coming together. Ever wondered why you adore someone's appearance but cringe the moment they speak? It's because the audible interaction didn't hit that sweet spot of constructive interference. That's where the real magic happens or doesn't, determining if it's true love or just a fleeting infatuation. Imagine this cosmic twist: if the audible interaction were also a hit, your love score would skyrocket to 200/200. It's a sonic confirmation that seals another part of the deal.

This phenomenon sheds light on why we connect to certain tunes while despising some of the most popular songs – sound waves are just energetic frequencies we hear. When they sync up perfectly, we're hooked; if not, it's a hard pass, no matter the song's popularity.

So, what a person sounds like isn't just background noise; it's a magnetic force that can pull you in. Think about blind dates – you hear someone on the phone without peeking at them, and suddenly, you're smitten with their voice. But here's the kicker: for the love story to truly take off, other variables of the matrix, too, need to chime in positively. It's a cosmic recipe; attraction doesn't happen out of thin air. There's a whole science behind it, turning attraction into a beautiful symphony. Here's the real deal: every sense in your arsenal plays a role in this cosmic connection. How someone looks, sounds, even smells – it all conspires to draw you in. Take that unique body scent, the pheromones dancing in the air; it's not just a subtle nuance. On a date, it might be masked with perfume, but once you get a bit closer, you'll catch a whiff of their true essence.

The magic happens when you smell something. It's not just a pleasant aroma; it's a journey to the receptors in your nose, converting into a signal – yes, another frequency playing into the matrix.

So, let's say you've got someone scoring a perfect 100 visually and another 100 for their voice, but if their scent and pheromones clash with your frequency, it becomes a cosmic hiccup – bringing down the score on your love matrix. That's the intricate dance of attraction, where every sense has a vote in the cosmic opus.

Dive into the intricacies of taste, and you'll find it's a make-or-break factor in a relationship. Picture this: when you kiss your partner, you're not just in the realm of touch; you're tasting and smelling them. It's a cosmic chemistry experiment. Depending on where you fall on the pH scale, certain tastes can either elevate the connection or send it spiraling down. If their taste aligns with your preference, it's a multiplier for your love, a constructive interaction that solidifies the next bond.

Moving on, let's talk about a realm where every variable of the matrix comes into play – sex. It's a metaphysical spectacle, a cosmic meeting involving the visual, the audible, the smell, the taste, the touch – more than half the entire matrix in action. Yet, despite its undeniable role, it's a misconception to label sex as the be-all and end-all of a relationship. It's just one note in the grand symphony of cosmic connections.

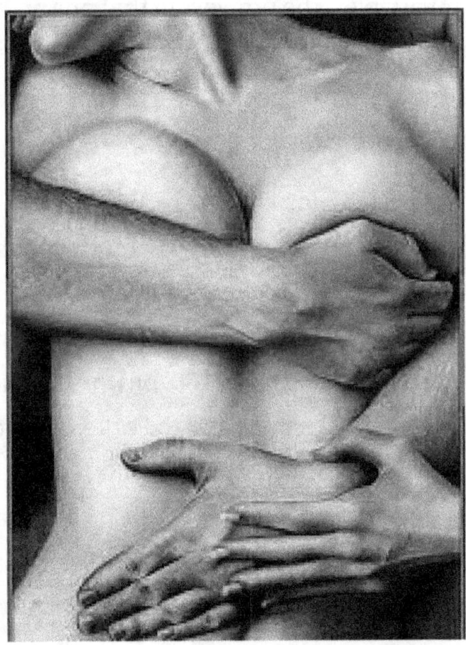

It's a common misconception that great sex is the linchpin holding a relationship together, but the reality is more complex. Exceptional intimacy doesn't guarantee a lasting connection. In many cases, when sex stands out as the sole highlight, the overall matrix score might be lacking. This makes for a shaky foundation where only the physical aspect holds things in place. In this instance, the visual attraction is 100, but the scent is-50, the voice or sound is-100, and the sex is 100, leaving one partner a score of 50 points total out of a possible 1000.

As the relationship continues, confusion sets in, and individuals ponder what went wrong. Often, the culprit is relying solely on sex to sustain a connection. We've all heard tales of someone being in a relationship just for the physical aspect — minimal communication, no emotional connection — yet they stick around for the deed. It's because, despite the average score in other matrix variables, the prowess in that one arena keeps the flame flickering, albeit temporarily. It's a cautionary tale that underscores the importance of a balanced matrix for a relationship to stand the test of time.

In unfortunate scenarios, the one receiving a high score in the relationship matrix often endures abuse but remains entangled, convinced that the abuser is the epitome of love because the abuser might have a 100 on visual attraction but-50 on the scent,-100 on the voice or sound and 100 on the sex, leaving that partner with a score of 50 points, and the other partner may have a perfect 100 on the visual, scent, sound and sex making it a total of 400 points, and so forth, creating a distorted reality for the victim. Therefore, despite the same love being reciprocated, it becomes a one-sided narrative because the victim has a high relationship matrix score; it gives them the promise that they have found their soulmate. On the other hand, their partner only has a relationship matrix of 50 points, and it is the high sex score that keeps the relationship going. It is this one-sided narrative that can lead to abuse of the person with the high score because when the partner with the low score starts the abuse, the partner with the high score endures it, be it verbal, mental, or even physical abuse, because their high score tells them that this is what love is, so they stay in an abusive relationship.

These metaphysical attributes intricately stabilize the relationship or, as the matrix calculations, overshadow the imbalance. It forms a formidable barrier to intervention; despite the well-intentioned advice to leave, the victim remains steadfast.

It's only when a realization dawns that their compatibility is fundamentally skewed and the two should not be together that the possibility of breaking free gains traction. The matrix, though complex, can sometimes be the key to unlocking the chains of an unhealthy relationship.

All in all, you must remember that the thing needed to obtain the perfect relationship is a high matrix score for both parties. Apart from the usual sensory things, another one on the matrix is intellect. You have to be attracted to a person's intellect, be it a brain that loves working, calculating for nuclear physics, doing mathematics, financial forecasting, studying earth and science, or just a plain dog walker. Every person has a subject that really turns them on, and so, too, shall your partner be turned on by your intellect.

It is a misconception that all men love a dumb blonde; that is only the case with persons who have no morals and are just looking for an easy connection. Other cases could be that people with high IQs love to be with a person who has a lower IQ only to eliminate the jealousy of competition. No couple should be in a competition with their mate; that is a recipe for disaster.

Ask yourself this question: what subject turns you on or keeps your interest? Whatever it is, will help you in choosing a partner and later maintain a healthy relationship with them. This is why, when taking the relationship questionnaire, all your answers must be truthful. It does not matter what other people think of your partner's occupation or education; only your opinion matters. Next on the list is activities; yes, that's right, what you do is another part of the matrix.

You and your partner need to be interested in the same type of activities, be it working out, watching movies, going to a comedy club, and laughing. It doesn't have to be the same thing entirely; if both of you like to work out, then one might like lifting weights and the other jogging. As long as it's something to keep both of you active, it could be anything like going bowling, camping, swimming, or even playing bingo.

You must keep active or on the go for a healthy relationship. Don't get me wrong, even taking naps in the middle of the day to enjoy a little afternoon delight is an activity. The key goal here is to keep moving or participating in activities that can help you as a couple to keep evolving; remember, without change, you can become stagnant, which can erode the foundation of your relationship.

Another part of the matrix is the personality of a person as a whole. When you take a long look at people, you will notice a variety of personalities. Most people want to be serious all the time, while others are playful and don't take things seriously. That's why your mate's personality plays a key role in keeping the relationship long-lasting.

For instance, I am the playful and intellectual type when it comes to science, whereas my partner is more serious, clean, and is fond of book reading, poetry, and art.

My playfulness rubs off on her, making life more enjoyable. I ground her with humor, and she helps me stay involved in the art world and so on.

You just have to be the yin to their yang, and balance and harmony will ensue. Nobody knows what combination of personalities is good for you except for you, so choose wisely. Life doesn't have to be dry and serious; when you are too serious, harbor problems and all the other issues during life, it can make you ill and sick. Therefore, taking a day trip to the beach or watching the stars at night will shed the sickness that life brings. Well, you won't do it yourself, but having such a partner who has such interests will bring the light to your dark life.

Last but not the least is your Bio-Ethereal Frequency. It is the final piece of the matrix. It will determine if you are a simple or a multifarious person. What I mean by that is when you examine a frequency, it could have either 1 or 10,000 wavelengths that make up that specific frequency, so a simple person may have a Bio-Ethereal frequency with only 1-5 wavelengths, whereas on the other hand, a multifarious person may have a Bio-Ethereal Frequency with 100-10,000 wavelengths that make up their Bio-Ethereal Frequency.

It means that the person with a simple B.E.F can only have a couple of soulmate matches or the person to spend eternity with and enjoy every minute of the relationship, which realistically is like playing the lotto because that person is going to have a hard time finding the perfect match. It doesn't mean that a simple person will not find a mate because you have to remember that there are different degrees of a relationship. For instance, you may have only scored 550 points for the total matrix, whereas your mate scored 750, but if you compromise on the things that don't really matter to make the relationship work, it might be enough for both of you for a long-lasting relationship.

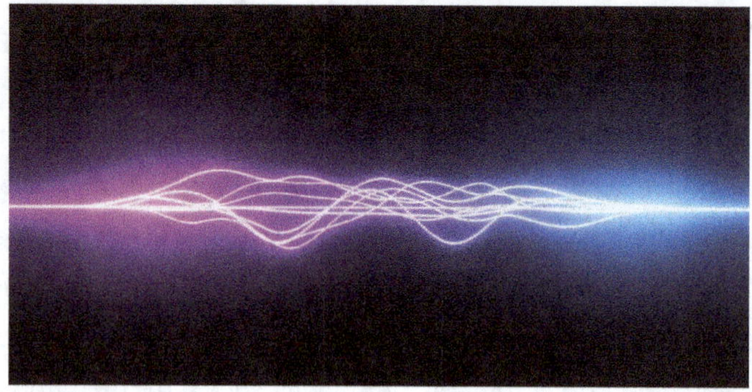

Contrary to that, a multifarious person can have 1000-25,000 wavelengths that make up their B.E.F., which means it is a lot easier for this person to have numerous friends and partners because they form a positive connection with almost everyone they meet. Because of this, almost anyone can be their soulmate, with whom they can form a relationship that will last a long time. Don't get me wrong, even a multifarious person will still have to compromise on some things, just not as much as a simple person would have to do to obtain the same kind of relationship.

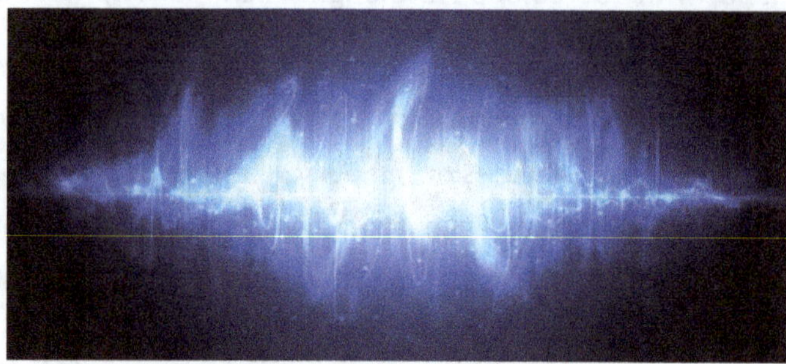

To have the complete matrix, you will have to have an in-person evaluation to obtain the scan for a total score. The good thing is that the Bio-Ethereal Frequency is like a fingerprint, meaning it can't be copied. Thus, the Bio-Ethereal Frequency can be measured and will complete the matrix for you.

With that being said, it turns out that when they talk about there being someone for everybody, it might not be the person you're currently with, but rest assured that there is somebody out there for you. The key is to assess potential life partners carefully, using the matrix as your guiding compass. Your soulmate could very well be someone boasting a substantial 1000 score on the matrix.

Individuals with a broader spectrum find it considerably easier to find a compatible match. They can resonate with a higher number of individuals in the population, widening their chances of encountering that elusive soulmate. In contrast, those with a limited number of frequencies face a more selective pool, making the partner search a tad more challenging.

Hence, unlocking the secret to a lasting relationship isn't a single revelation but a dynamic interplay of multiple variables forming the matrix. In simple terms, the higher the score on that matrix, the more enduring the relationship tends to be. That gut feeling warning you against dating someone? It might just be your inner self picking up on their matrix score, signaling that this person might not be the ideal plus one for you.

My journey into the realm of bio-ethereal frequency was serendipitous. During a class where we crafted our own transducers, I stumbled upon a fascinating phenomenon. When I connected my transducer to an oscilloscope, I noticed a signal even before attaching the other leads. Intriguingly, the signal vanished when I let go, only to reappear when I grabbed it again. To explore further, I had a classmate take hold of the leads, unveiling a mysterious unison of frequencies. It was a chance discovery that opened the door to understanding the unseen forces shaping our connections. In a moment of revelation, the signal returned, but with a unique signature for each individual. As I repeated the experiment with different classmates, it dawned on me that this signal wasn't a random occurrence but a product of the person holding the leads. I coined it the bio-ethereal frequency, an emanation from within. In a world where external appearances can be masked, this internal frequency remains a genuine expression of an individual. And what better way to tap into its potential than testing it through the matrix?

So, behold the secret to enduring relationships – it's not some elusive mystery but a matter of scoring high on the matrix. It's not about the physical act of intimacy; it's about the amalgamation of energies and frequencies. Now armed with the knowledge of the bio-ethereal frequency and the matrix, you hold the key to deciphering the unseen forces that shape lasting connections. It turns out the answer was never hidden in the realm of physicality but in the combination of frequencies and variables that form the foundation of a relationship.

Chapter 5: Purpose of Life

Life kicks off as a tiny spark in our parent's eyes, just a mix of matter and energy. This grand journey is all about discovery. Picture it as the first chapter of a book called "Discovery."

As kids, we often dream of becoming doctors, lawyers, or firefighters. It's like setting out on a quest to uncover our true selves. What makes us tick? What are we passionate about? These are the mysteries we navigate in the early chapters of our lives.

The bigger picture of life's purpose remains a bit of a puzzle. We don't have a roadmap telling us what we're supposed to do or who we're meant to be with. So, the adventure begins with understanding ourselves—the "Discovery" chapter—where we peel back the layers and uncover the essence of who we are.

As children, we often declare lofty ambitions—dreams of becoming doctors, lawyers, policemen, or firefighters. It's a reflection of our innate desire to covet, to absorb the essence of things that appeal to us, and perhaps, to become a part of them.

However, these early aspirations shouldn't be dismissed lightly. They are a glimpse into our instinctual desire to explore and make our own mark on the world. It's like wanting to become something that captivates us.

Yet, life is a journey of experimentation. Many times, we need to try out different roles, professions, and aspects of authority to discover who we truly are. It's a process of self-discovery, navigating through the maze of possibilities.

There's wisdom in letting life take the wheel. By allowing ourselves to flow with the current of experiences, we often find ourselves guided in the direction we are meant to be on our unique path. In these moments of exploration and acceptance, we uncover the layers of our authentic selves, gradually steering toward the destination that aligns with our true essence. You might label it a life path or perhaps conjure up your own term for it.

My journey toward self-awareness began around the age of 18, a pivotal moment akin to someone flicking on a switch, illuminating the path ahead. I was never the math or science whiz; those subjects never held my interest. Instead, a fervent passion for innovation and a longing to create things simmered within me. Then, one day, it happened – as if a light had suddenly flooded my awareness.

My academic record is far from adorned with high achievements. I never graduated high school and never received any notable honors. Perhaps, in part, because I didn't exert much effort – I was too busy searching for the essence of who I truly was. Those were the years of self-discovery, where formal education took a backseat to the journey of understanding myself and finding the path that resonated with my authentic aspirations.

So, in my earlier years, I wore many hats – the class clown, the jock, even the occasional flirt trying to charm the ladies. I was exploring different facets of life, attempting to grasp what resonated with me. However, it wasn't until a twist of fate led me to summer school, a bid to fulfill graduation requirements, that I found myself on an unexpected path.

I entered an introductory class to NDT (Non-Destructive Testing), where I delved into ultrasound, radiography, magnetic particle testing, and a labyrinth of technical jargon that often eludes comprehension. Despite my past indifference to subjects like physics and astronomy, something clicked in this class. I began to see how the seemingly disparate aspects of life intertwined, overlapping in intricate patterns.

This revelation unfolded through the lens of science, a discipline that offered a unique perspective. Whether exploring emotions, light, music, or a person's essence, each element is interconnected with the others.

Science became the thread stitching together the fabric of existence. It's a concept at the heart of our discussion in this book—the book of origin, where every facet of life converges into a beautiful and harmonious mosaic.

If you're tuned into what I'm expressing here, that light should be flickering to life within you because this realization served as the pivotal key—the very essence of everything, the crux of life itself. It became the compass guiding me to self-awareness, defining not only what I am but who I am meant to be.

As I inched closer to my aspirations, an undeniable shift occurred. It was as if an invincible force enveloped me, rendering me impervious to setbacks. Vibrant energy pulsed through my veins, casting a positive glow on every endeavor. Confidence became my constant companion, fueling my journey.

However, I'll admit there were moments when I veered off course. Success brought with it a subtle challenge—an inflating ego, a head slightly swelling beyond its boundaries. It's a delicate dance, recognizing the fine line between self-assuredness and unchecked pride. Yet, in these moments of reflection, I found the balance necessary to stay on the right track, ensuring that the radiance of positive energy continued to illuminate my path.

So, as I embraced success, I found myself unwittingly transforming into a self-proclaimed "ladies' man," convinced I could conquer anything—essentially, a miniature deity in my own narrative. Yet, this shift marked a departure from my true path. The more I strayed, the more I attracted negative energy and encountered a series of unfortunate events.

In the midst of this deviation, I spiraled into a bout of depression, contemplating the weight of my existence and the impact of my absence on those around me. It's a dark space that, regrettably, many of us navigate at some point in life.

This is where the metaphor of letting life take the wheel gains significance. During bouts of confusion, depression, or when an avalanche of negative energy descends upon us, it often signifies that we're veering away from our destiny. It's a wake-up call to realign with our true path.

Once you find yourself on that right track, gazing destiny squarely in the eyes, the shift is profound. The energy that surges through you, the sense of bliss—it's unparalleled. It's the euphoria of being in sync with your destiny and stands as the most incredible high in the world.

Remember, the purpose of life transcends individual identity and personal goals, much like the synergy of worker ants collaborating for a common cause. Humans are inherently social creatures, reliant on a collective, a unit of individuals destined to come together. In the unity of these individuals, there exists an unstoppable force capable of turning aspirations into reality, ensuring positivity prevails in their endeavors. So, while discovering who you are remains paramount, it's equally vital to recognize the importance of your group, your unit, and your counterparts. This collaborative force, when united, possesses the strength to overcome any obstacle and manifest their collective visions into reality.

Now, taking a step back, the journey of self-discovery involves tuning into what truly brings you pleasure. It's not merely about chasing a high-paying job but about aligning with what resonates with your inner self, what fuels your passion. This nuanced approach ensures that not only do you thrive individually, but your collective unit also flourishes, creating a harmonious blend of personal fulfillment and shared success. Absolutely, the pursuit of happiness transcends the allure of high-paying jobs with impressive titles. A job offering six, seven, or even eight figures might seem enticing, but money alone doesn't equate to genuine fulfillment. In fact, wealth often brings its own set of challenges.

So, it's crucial not to view jobs through the lens of status, income, or hierarchical power dynamics. Life is not about the title you hold, the money you make, or the number of people you can command. The essence of life lies in giving and sharing, in making connections with others to collectively create something wonderful.

The first step in this journey is understanding what truly brings you pleasure. By identifying your sources of joy, you can begin to define your function in the grand orchestration of existence. If working with animals brings you joy, perhaps your calling is to be a veterinarian or to contribute as a helper in a veterinary setting. It's about aligning your passion with your role, fostering a sense of purpose that extends beyond individual success to contribute meaningfully to the world around you.

Rescuing animals might seem unconventional as a life purpose, but consider the profound impact it can have. Your act of rescuing an animal might be the lifeline for someone who, through their connection with that creature, finds solace, clarity, and the ability to think clearly. It's a ripple effect where the joy derived from saving an animal transcends its immediate impact, potentially influencing the discovery of innovative ideas and even contributing to breakthroughs in fields like cancer research.

Similarly, if you're inclined toward mechanics, your role might extend beyond the traditional boundaries of fixing vehicles. Perhaps you're destined to be part of a group pioneering a new era of alternative vehicles. Your unique perspective and input could be the missing piece that propels the collective toward success.

The key, once again, lies in identifying what gives you pleasure. This self-awareness helps define your function in life. It positions you to be an integral part of the puzzle alongside your counterparts. This collaborative effort, fueled by individual passions and strengths, harmoniously assembles to create a bigger picture—a purpose that goes beyond personal satisfaction and contributes meaningfully to the complex web of life.

Once you've defined your function and understood what brings you pleasure, the next crucial step is to be attuned to your counterparts. These counterparts could be a diverse group—a banker, a mathematician, and a physicist collaborating on groundbreaking financial innovations. Alternatively, it might be a seemingly ordinary duo, like a house mom with a penchant for gardening joining forces with an engineering-inclined gardener. Together, this unlikely pair could pioneer an organic alternative power source, showcasing the boundless possibilities when diverse skills converge.

Your counterparts are not confined to a specific mold; the potential combinations are limitless. However, recognizing them requires an openness to external conversations and stimuli. Engaging with people beyond your immediate sphere can lead to serendipitous encounters with those who complement your skills and perspectives.

Moreover, trust your instincts when interacting with new individuals. That funny feeling might not be a signal for a romantic entanglement but rather an intuitive nudge that this person could be a valuable counterpart. Embracing diverse connections expands the potential of your collaborative efforts, unlocking a vast array of possibilities for creative innovation and impactful contributions to the world.

When connecting with potential counterparts, treat them as individuals engaged in a shared journey of discovery. Engage in conversations that unveil their passions, skills, and unique perspectives, allowing them to reciprocate the process. As you delve into these interactions, you'll sense a natural fit when you've encountered the right group. Positive energy will flow, indicating that you're on the right path, even if the connection isn't necessarily of a romantic or emotional nature. Once your counterparts are identified, envision life as a colossal machine, with each individual serving as a vital component. Whether it's a guy or a girl, the complexity lies in recognizing that within each person exists a multitude of other life forms, each living their own life to survive. These diverse aspects come together harmoniously to create a singular individual with the capacity to teach, create, or design.

This perspective illuminates the interconnectedness of life, emphasizing the intricate collaboration within each person. It underscores the collective nature of our existence, with each individual contributing their unique elements to the grand machinery of life.

When you contemplate humanity as a whole, encompassing billions of individuals, the overarching purpose is a collective pursuit of evolution. It transcends the cyclical patterns of mundane existence—working to pay bills, avoiding eviction, fueling a car for weekend activities. If one remains stuck in this repetitive loop, seeking only temporary pleasures without a broader perspective, it's akin to spinning wheels without substantial progress. The essence lies in shifting our mindset and recognizing that we are integral parts of a more extensive, interconnected machinery. The ultimate goal is evolution, propelling us beyond the monotony of mere survival. The danger lies in getting ensnared in routines that lack growth, where time is spent until life's conclusion.

Life is more than the sum of these repetitive actions; it's a contribution to a greater whole. Anything that resists evolution, that refrains from change, risks stagnation. Analogous to water confined to a small space, it becomes stagnant, losing the vibrancy that once sustained life. In this stasis, what once nurtured life can turn septic, emphasizing the imperative nature of embracing change and evolution for the flourishing of individuals and the collective whole.

Likening life to a river or stream is a profound analogy. Just as a body of water that keeps moving never goes stagnant and continually creates life, people, too, should avoid stagnation. Remaining dynamic and embracing change is the essence of sustaining life and growth.

Stagnation, whether in water or life, leads to decay and eventual demise. To avoid this fate, we must embrace the big picture—the next chapter in the purpose of life, which once again centers around evolution. It involves individuals coming together, working collectively toward a shared goal, with the ultimate aim of becoming the best version of homo sapiens possible.

Consider our evolutionary journey—from Neanderthals and cavemen to the present. The big picture involves striving for continuous improvement and aspiring to transcend our current state. As life progresses, who knows what lies beyond? Perhaps neo-sapiens or ultra-sapiens. Our DNA continues to ascend a couple of chains, and the goal is to evolve. It's about contributing to the larger mosaic of human evolution and embracing the ever-unfolding chapters of our shared story.

Indeed, the big picture involves small groups of people uniting under a common goal—an overarching purpose that propels the advancement of the human race. As we transition to the next chapter, a critical goal emerges: liberating ourselves from the shackles of hydrocarbon-burning fossil fuels that dominate our cars and transportation systems.

It's time to usher in a new era, embracing sustainable alternatives like electric or nuclear power. However, this is not the conventional nuclear power associated with power plants, as it's widely acknowledged that a significant portion of the energy produced is wasted as heat.

True progress lies in exploring compact, efficient solutions—tiny pieces of uranium, iridium, or cobalt, each holding immense energy potential. A minuscule, eraser-sized fragment of these elements could power a vehicle for an extended period, ranging from 75 days to three years solely on electricity. The challenge lies not in the lack of technological potential but in our own stagnation.

As we propel ourselves toward the future, the big picture involves breaking free from the inertia that has held us back. It's about acknowledging the potential for revolutionary advancements and channeling our collective efforts into steering humanity toward a sustainable and progressive future.

Our collective potential is hindered when the currents of innovative thought aren't flowing in the right direction. For society to advance and thrive in a cleaner, pollution-free environment, it's imperative that we break free from stagnant patterns. This leap forward is not just about improving our immediate surroundings; it's about preparing ourselves to explore other planets, encounter diverse life forms, and unravel the mysteries of other galaxies.

The consequences of remaining stagnant on Earth are stark—we risk self-destruction through war or succumb to unforeseen genetic diseases. The urgency lies in transcending our limitations, opening ourselves up to positive external influences, and allowing life to steer us toward progress.

Recognizing when you're on the right track is crucial. Positive energy becomes a beacon, signaling alignment with your purpose. Letting life take hold of the wheel and welcoming external influences in a positive manner becomes a transformative process. This journey of self-awareness is a gradual one as you navigate through experiences and connections. Just as I am seeking my counterparts, this book serves as a contribution to the collective pool of knowledge, aiming to inspire others to become self-aware and positive contributors to the evolution of humanity.

In this endeavor, each individual who becomes self-aware becomes a positive force, contributing to the evolution pool and collectively shaping a better world for the human race. It's about fostering a shared consciousness that propels us toward a future where positive change is not just a possibility but an inevitability.

Chapter 6: Heaven and Hell

In this chapter, we'll uncover the cosmic story of Heaven and Hell. Imagine the Almighty not as a judgmental referee but as the ultimate cosmic coach, cheering you on in your journey of self-discovery. Let's break free from the traditional script, envisioning a universe where you craft your own heavenly existence.

Now, let's explore uncharted cosmic realms where heaven isn't a freebie but the hard-earned trophy of your work well done. Envision ethereal rewards not as handouts but as the fruits of your labor.

Hold on as we embark on a mind-bending voyage where life isn't a random gift but the grand prize for your cosmic grind. Forget about giving it away; savor every twist and turn, finding purpose in the chaotic dance of existence.

Fellow cosmic wanderer, get ready as we delve into celestial philosophy, transcending the mundane. Let's rewrite the cosmic narrative and redefine what Heaven and Hell truly mean in this interstellar adventure.

As we navigate the celestial landscapes of Heaven and Hell, let's parallel the wild ride of religion shaping our earthly mindset. Questioning the conventional divine script, it's time for a laid-back examination of how religion has played its own game of control throughout history.

No more pretending it's all about prayers and hymns; religion has been a heavyweight in the control arena. Leaders flexing their authority, societies sticking to the script – it's been a real cosmic chess match. Ponder the self-made heavens and the hard work behind ethereal reward, and let's toss religion into the mix.

In a universe where religion isn't merely a Sunday sermon but a tool justifying authority and societal rules, it has steered the ship of society for ages. Let's open the conversation, rethink the entire dynamic, and give our views on religion a fresh perspective. Here's to keeping it real in both celestial and earthly realms – a cosmic chat transcending the mundane, sparking new thoughts. Let's tie this conversation to the earthly wisdom shared about rules and free will. If we're reimagining the divine script, let's view it as a galactic parenting gig. Just as a parent sets rules for a child to grow into a good person, perhaps religion does the same on a grand cosmic scale. Consider this: if the Almighty granted us free will, it doesn't make sense for Him to impose restrictive rules. Imagine the Almighty as a parent letting their child loose in the world after establishing some ground rules. The rules weren't meant to chain us but to be tools for developing good judgment and character.

Let's mull over the idea that religion, the Ten Commandments, and such were like a group of people trying to bring order to the chaos. It's not about stifling free will; it's about maintaining checks and balances so the playground doesn't turn into utter mayhem.

In this exploration of the divine and earthly realms, we're keeping it real, pondering parallels between rules and earthly guidelines. Here's to the cosmic parenting playbook, where free will and a bit of order dance together in the grand waltz.

Bringing this discussion back to Earth, let's explore the intricate dance between religion, free will, and societal evolution. Using religion as a control tool is like instilling the "fear of God" to make folks think twice before venturing into murky waters. In this Universal dialogue, the Bible becomes a guidebook, not a rigid life script to be blindly followed.

Here's the twist: living life strictly by the book might squash the very free will God intended for us. It's about balancing the scales, embracing free will and independent thought while recognizing the societal intelligence that keeps us thriving as a community.

In our society, evolution has guided us to understand the delicate dance of societal norms, ensuring growth and harmony rather than a free-for-all. While you can go rogue, there are consequences – a catch to consider.

Biblical phrases aren't handcuffs but clues guiding us on a true path. As we sift through ancient verses, we're not shackling ourselves but seeking wisdom to navigate this maze. Buckle up for the next leg of our journey, decoding clues and balancing free will with the wisdom of the ages.

In this belief, life on Earth is the ultimate gift, a vacation amidst the millennia of universal work entrusted to us – a task of maintaining balance in the vast cosmic dance.

Returning to the phrase, "on earth as it is in heaven," it's not a call to perfection but an invitation to carry the good we do here into the celestial beyond. Picture it as packing our suitcase with the positive energy generated during our earthly escapade.

Remember, we're dual beings – matter and energy. As the cosmic playbook reminds us, energy can't be created or destroyed, only transformed. In this dance of molecules and universal energy, the Almighty isn't just a spectator but the very essence that binds everything together.

The Creator isn't just omnipotent and omnipresent; The Creator is the intelligent energy knitting the molecules of air, earth, sand, and water together. Whether a rock crystal or a flowing river, it's all part of this cosmic symphony. In this chapter of exploration, let's unravel the threads connecting us to the intelligent energy permeating the very fabric of the universe.

Delve further into cosmic intricacies, where the energy orchestrating the cosmic dance is nothing less than the essence of the Almighty – a cosmic power grid maintaining order among myriad molecules and matter. Everything, from rocks to rivers, is part of this divine energy –is the Creator in dynamic action.

The fascinating part is that as our earthly chapter concludes, we transition into electricity – an energy form. Remember, energy doesn't vanish; it transforms. Picture this transition as merging into the white light, not a tunnel but a return to our origin – pure energy.

Brace yourself for the cosmic speed limit. Energy moves at an astonishing 186,000 miles per second and thought could rival that speed. In a blink of an eye, you could be up to 186,000 miles away.

Within this vast cosmic expanse, there's a complex choreography of molecular structures, each requiring energy to bind them together. When we talk about reconnecting with loved ones beyond the earthly realm, it's not just sentiment- it's a reunion of positive energies amassed throughout our cosmic journey.

Contemplating the nature of energy and its velocities leads to intriguing possibilities. Frequencies vary, with mundane speeds like 734 mph contrasting the extraordinary 186,000 miles per second of light. The question arises: in the afterlife, where might we find ourselves in this cosmic continuum? Could we traverse vast distances in the blink of an eye?

Consider a conceptual "heaven" as the interstitial space between points A and B, composed of matter and structure held together by energy. Picture it as a cosmic spider web, each line connecting to a point in time, a fragment of someone's memory. In this expansive landscape, we encounter shared memories with everyone we've crossed paths with – a profound opportunity to revisit those moments with depth and connection beyond the earthly realm. When we talk about reconnecting with loved ones beyond the earthly realm, it's not just sentiment- it's a reunion of positive energies amassed throughout our cosmic journey.

We're not merely discussing the end of life; we're contemplating a dynamic transition where energy reunites with the universal dance. The rendezvous with companions is an integral part of this cosmic ballet.

Let's dive deeper into the cosmic essence, where the Almighty isn't just a concept but the omnipresent energy holding everything together – from steel to rocks, water, and air molecules. It's the fabric of everything that is and ever will be, making the Almighty both the Alpha and the Omega, encompassing all.

We see Water, Glass, Carbon, Steel and other substances like this,

But on an atomic scale, they and everything else looks like this,

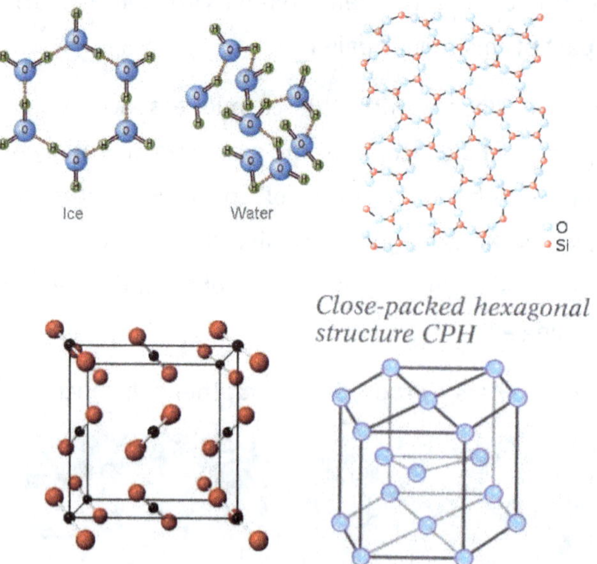

The Water, glass, carbon, steel and even the space between them share valance electron, that's how it works on an atomic level. Now you can see that everything that exists is in contact with everything in the cosmos no matter how far the distance; on an atomic scale, we are all connected, and we share the same energy.

Now you should be getting the big picture, that heaven is all of the positive and happy emotions, love, and adventure that all life forms had and will have experienced will live on eternal for all to visit and experience.

Consider this concept: the omniscience of the Almighty isn't tied to a single go-around. In the cosmic journey, we might have lived countless lives, in different forms, on various planets, though perhaps a million Big Bangs.

In this vast space, every possible outcome may have already played out, making the Creator's all-knowing nature a reflection of the timeless repetitions in the cosmic saga. Looping back to our cosmic exploration of "on earth as it is in heaven," merging science and religion suggests that energy cannot be destroyed, turning cherished memories from our earthly sojourns into building blocks for our cosmic heaven. In this perspective, heaven and hell aren't separate realms but facets of the same space. There's no tug-of-war between the Almighty and the devil- it's a unified energy field.

As we ponder this cosmic dance, remember that we're intertwining the threads of science, religion, and the unknown.

In this realm, it boils down to a dance between good and evil, a universal tango where we wield the free will to choose our steps. Some embrace the light, others the shadows, and then there are those who opt for neutrality, seemingly avoiding the dance altogether by doing nothing.

Yet, here's the twist: even in the dance of good and evil, our choices ripple beyond our earthly existence. The notion of forgiveness becomes a salve by releasing that negative energy, that heavy burden of hate; we give it back to the one who wronged us. It's an equilibrium where choosing forgiveness becomes a pathway to liberation.

Now, imagine this: the more we forgive those who've caused us pain, the richer our heaven becomes when our earthly journey concludes.

It's a cosmic savings account of love and positive emotion that we carry into the beyond. In this experience, we're not just discussing emotions and forgiveness; we're building a pattern of cause and effect. So, fellow voyager, let's keep twirling through the dance of emotions, forgiveness, and the unknown. Now, picture this journey where time isn't linear, and you can revisit moments in time, like being a carefree kid and sharing a day with your mom in the cosmic heaven. Her energy persists – it doesn't die. This perpetual energy dance connects us to those we've loved and lost. But here's the twist: the journey doesn't end with a single lifetime.

Passing on in this earthly chapter brings a new responsibility, a duty that might span millennia before our energy is recycled into a fresh existence. This responsibility involves the diligence of holding molecules together across galaxies and the vast expanse of the universe.

Now, let's question the notion of Judgment Day, where God supposedly sorts the "Book of Life." It seems like a tale spun to maintain control, a narrative suggesting that God is unforgiving in nature. However, the notion that God sits in judgment seems made up to me.

With the gift of free will, we become the architects of our own judgments. It's not about God forgiving or condemning; it's about the self-reflection born from our choices.

Consider this: for those immersed in cruelty and unrepentant in their actions, the karmic consequences are profound. If you've reveled in causing pain and torture, death doesn't bring redemption. Instead, you carry the legacy of your deeds into the beyond – no heaven, just the haunting echoes of hate, anguish, and torture

Moving on to implications, souls tormented by the hell they have created may disrupt the cosmic dance, leading to unstable situations in atomic structures. The duty functions they were meant to sustain are compromised by the turmoil they carry, allowing molecules to roam where they shouldn't. We're not just exploring the consequences of our actions; we're delving into the intricate dance of energy, choices, and the cosmic order.

Our actions always have an impact of our actions on the fabric of the universe. While not a destructive force, the repercussions of one's deeds can lead to a cosmic event, reshaping the known universe as we understand it.

Now, onto the concept of repentance. It's not a mere verbal plea for forgiveness; it requires a deep acknowledgment of the wrongs committed, seeking forgiveness not just from a higher power but from the souls affected. For true redemption, the forgiveness of those you've wronged becomes the catalyst for a transformation. It doesn't erase the past, but it injects a small bit of love, hope, and compassion into your cosmic legacy, potentially sustaining you in the performance of your cosmic duty. When it comes to the elusive Judgment Day, there's no need for fear, for God doesn't sit in judgment; we are the architects of our own judgment. So, in departing this earthly realm, the path to the best heaven involves not just following biblical rules but embodying the fundamental principle of treating others as you'd want to be treated. It's about going the extra mile to help your fellow beings, weaving threads of compassion and understanding into the fabric of existence.

In this journey, the ultimate sacrifice is not just giving away the shirt off your back but being willing to give your life for another. It's an act of profound love, a camaraderie that transcends boundaries and plays a crucial role in creating your own heaven.

The principle here is clear: the more you give to others, the more you receive in return. It's not just a karmic exchange; it's akin to the enduring love and emotional bonds you share with your parents. That emotional connection, that feeling of shared pain and joy, extends beyond the earthly realm, creating a bond for eternity.

Now, consider expanding this emotional bond beyond your family to encompass your fellow humans. By doing your best to look out for others, you increase your chances of crafting the best cosmic heaven. It's about performing ethereal duties with compassion and kindness, ensuring that the energy within you continues its celestial dance until the time comes for a new spiritual adventure.

For example, Oskar Schindler saved over 1,200 Jews because he felt that something needed to be done, and those he saved had children that were told the story of Mr. Schindler and so on, and today more than 7,000 people are alive because of his actions and all the love from those 7,000 people gave rise to the positive energy that Oskar will receive in the afterlife.

As we segue into the next chapters, exploring the nuances of universes and spiritual rebirths, one thing is clear: creating your own heaven is no walk in the park. It demands hard work, selflessness, and a commitment to the camaraderie that binds us all. So, fellow cosmic traveler, let's keep navigating these celestial waters and discovering the secrets of the cosmos.

Let's debunk the notion of heaven as a leisurely retreat amidst fluffy clouds. Instead, heaven emerges as the most challenging endeavor you'll ever face in your existence. It demands unwavering strength, boundless love, and the dedication of all cosmic entities working together.

Let's refocus on our theoretical purpose – the driving force of evolution. As we delve into its origin, a fundamental principle emerges: everything is built on the foundation of evolving, recycling, and contributing to the next civilization.

Consider the intricate dance of DNA, a code capable of retaining intelligence. As energy is recycled into new souls, we witness extraordinary individuals like Bach, Einstein, Oppenheimer, and savants who showcase incredible abilities from a young age, often without formal education. This phenomenon is a result of DNA intricately woven into the fabric of energy.

Here's the twist: the purpose of this DNA isn't just personal; it's to help societies on various planets transition from primitive states to advanced civilizations. It guides the evolution of cultures – from fine arts to mechanics to the complexities of war.

In the journey, embracing the entirety of existence becomes the key. Evolution, love for our fellow beings, and shedding the shackles of hate and torture are essential steps. By transforming life on Earth into a semblance of heaven, we pave the way for an even greater heaven in the afterlife, enriched by the lessons learned during our-odyssey.

Let's not forget: life is a gift, a reward for the tireless work of intelligent energy maintaining the universe's organization. The duality of good and bad, the negative aspects, and unstable atoms play a crucial role in generating energy. This naturally occurring energy once harnessed and understood, can be a force for the greater good, propelling our civilization forward. Consider the possibilities of tapping into the atom itself, unlocking trillions of terawatts of energy per second stored within a cube centimeter of radioactive material. This breakthrough would not only revolutionize our energy sources but also empower us to travel to other planets with alternative propulsion systems. It's a leap, fueled by the understanding and cultivation of natural energies, that can propel us toward a future of boundless possibilities and exploration.

This is the big picture, the essence of existence – embracing evolution, cultivating love, and transcending negativity. Life on Earth, a treasured gift, serves as our canvas for learning and growth. Navigating this cosmic odyssey, we discern the delicate balance between good and bad, harnessing energies for untold possibilities.

It's a profound journey where lessons contribute to the evolution of civilizations, laying the groundwork for a cosmic afterlife. So, fellow traveler, let's navigate the unknown realms of the universe with understanding, compassion, and unbridled curiosity.

Chapter 7: Conclusion

Take a moment to reflect on what we've explored and find comfort in the valuable insights we've gained. From the moment we awaken from sleep to the start of each new day, science guides our understanding of ourselves and the world around us.

Contemplate the grand interconnectedness of existence, where every tiny particle follows the cosmic dance.

We're all part of the same fabric, united by natural forces and universal laws.

As we delved further into scientific inquiry, we uncovered the timeless concepts of frequency, energy, and resonance.

These basic principles act as the underlying forces shaping our existence, shaping our realities, and guiding our progress.

Like the stars in the sky, we humans are made of the same cosmic materials. Evolution shapes us, allowing us to find our role in the grand story of existence, constantly changing and adjusting as time goes on.

Evolution is essential for progress, driving us forward in our quest for self-improvement and development. Without it, we would remain stagnant, missing out on the valuable contributions that diversity offers to our existence.

As we conclude our journey through science and its marvels, let's commit to carrying the torch of knowledge forward. Let's recognize the potential of science to guide us and enable us to craft a future brimming with opportunities.

In the vast expanse of the universe, we are simply ordinary players following the enduring patterns dictated by science. So, let us march forward with courage and conviction, for the journey ahead is filled with infinite promise and boundless potential.

Change is a constant force that drives progress. Stagnation hinders growth, creating inertia and stillness where nothing flourishes. Yet, within the dance of the cosmos, there exists a powerful guiding force: gravity.

Just as gravity orchestrates the movements of celestial bodies, it also influences the intricate dance of subatomic particles. Consider the humble atom, like H2O, the very essence of simplicity. Within its structure, electrons orbit protons in concentric rings, each layer holding a precise number of these fundamental particles. As molecules become more complex, the arrangement of electrons becomes more intricate, with each electron fulfilling its essential function to maintain molecular stability.

We notice similarities between small and large scales when we widen our perspective. In space, celestial objects follow rules of distance, bringing order to the vastness. This intelligent energy, this universal harmony, guides them in their cosmic ballet, ensuring balance and preventing catastrophe.

Reflecting on the universe's intricate design, we gain insight into the creation of gravity—a frequency that shapes the very fabric of existence. Like the ebb and flow of tides, this frequency wields both constructive and destructive potential, shaping the destiny of worlds and civilizations alike.

In our pursuit of spiritual understanding, we find ourselves immersed in a universal harmony that transcends the boundaries of race and belief. Spirituality serves as our guiding light on the journey of self-discovery and personal growth.

Embracing the constant flux of change, we recognize it as the heartbeat of life's most profound adventures. Through attunement with universal energies, we tap into the boundless potential within, charting a course toward fulfillment and enlightenment.

The essence of spirituality, as delineated in ancient texts, lies in its role as a catalyst for evolution. Our collective consciousness, comprised of memories stored as electrical impulses, spans across the vast expanse of time and space. Indeed, considering the multitude of galaxies beyond our own Milky Way, modern science underscores the interconnectedness of all existence.

In a galaxy where the sun is active, the potential for carbon-based life forms akin to ourselves arises at specific distances from that Sun. However, other planets at similar distances may exist where life takes on different forms, such as silicon- or methane-based organisms. These variations in elemental composition dictate the fundamental structure of life on those planets.

The human race, in this grand scheme, holds no inherent superiority. We experience life's myriad aspects—birth, death, love, and conflict—just as any other sentient beings might. Contemplating spirituality in this context suggests that life elsewhere possesses a similar essence or "soul," as it manifests energy within living entities.

It is believed that our experiences and actions shape our character, forming what we commonly call the "soul." This concept underscores how individuals develop into either kind or unkind adults. Remarkably, when we consider other planets, we can speculate that they, too, undergo similar developmental processes. However, there could be civilizations whose evolution is uniquely guided by mathematics. Every facet of existence may be intricately intertwined with mathematical principles on such a planet, potentially surpassing our understanding of mathematics here on Earth.

Conversely, elsewhere in the cosmos, there might exist a civilization whose foundation lies in science. This society could be continuously innovating, pioneering revolutionary scientific technologies with the potential to eradicate diseases like cancer and pioneer anti-aging solutions. Such diversity in the guiding principles of different civilizations throughout the universe highlights the vastness of possibilities and the potential for unfathomable advancements beyond our current comprehension.

Gravitational devices enable their vehicles to float effortlessly, accompanied by other sources of propulsion. Picture a race governed solely by music—a society where melodies possess the power to heal, uplift spirits, and even bring about demise. In this unique civilization, energy persists beyond death, echoing the interconnectedness of all existence.

In this cosmic tapestry, nothing truly vanishes; energy merely transforms and finds a new purpose. Technology is dispersed into the cosmos upon departure, ensuring its energy contributes to the universal cycle. Moments in time and experiences, eternal in their essence, become woven into the fabric of reality, enriching the cosmos with their presence.

With each cycle of rebirth, energy must be replenished, drawn from the reservoir of shared knowledge and experiences. This energy, infused with the essence of existence, carries a repository of information within it. Occasionally, there's a fascinating phenomenon—a bleed-through effect—where one may glimpse into another's life or tap into their knowledge, blurring the boundaries of individuality. Imagine the symphony of existence reverberating with the fusion of collective wisdom and interconnectedness. Within this vast orchestra, remarkable beings emerge, seemingly endowed with unparalleled talents. While we often attribute their brilliance to personal genius, it may well be a manifestation of the cosmic inheritance—lessons learned and insights gained across generations, echoing through the ages.

Think about déjà vu, that feeling like you've been there or done that before, even though logically, you know it's your first time. Maybe we're accessing some shared database of experiences, picking up snippets of what others have lived through across time. It's like every decision and outcome has been repeated, and during déjà vu, we're just getting a peek into other versions of reality overlapping with our own.

Now, let's talk about relationships—a domain where science and spirituality intersect intriguingly. Think of each person as a distinct frequency, an energetic fingerprint with its own rhythm.

Just like snowflakes, no two bio-ethereal frequencies are the same. Some resonate with a few frequencies, while others resonate with many possibilities.

This vibrant dance brings souls together, creating a connection that's hard to put into words. Have you ever felt an instant connection with someone, like you've known them forever? It's because your energies are aligning, coming together in a timeless and boundless way.

As you navigate life, remember that you're never on this journey alone. You're connected to a vast network of souls, all sharing experiences and knowledge. Embrace the mysteries that come your way, as they hold the answers to unlocking your full potential and finding balance in a universe full of opportunities.

In the intricate dance of life, our interactions with others are like the harmonies of a grand symphony, orchestrated by our unique Bio-ethereal frequencies. Love, hate, war—these manifestations of human connection are deeply intertwined with the resonance of our beings. Consider the pursuit of finding a soul mate, that elusive match where every note aligns perfectly. Yet, harmony is often disrupted when one's positive score clashes with another's negative frequencies, save for the realm of physical intimacy, where passion can sometimes cloud judgment.

If you're in a relationship like this, it's not your fault. It's just a matter of not being on the same page. Realizing this can help you move forward without blaming yourself and give you the strength to find a better match. Plenty of other people are out there, and with patience, you'll find someone right for you.

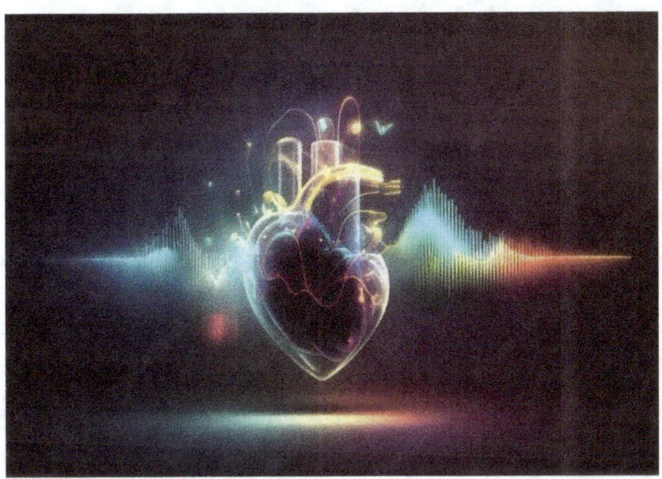

In matters of the heart, it's crucial to recognize that our Bio-ethereal frequencies influence our romantic entanglements and our sense of purpose. Without a clear purpose or goal, we might wander aimlessly, attempting to find satisfaction in temporary distractions or risky behaviors. Rest assured, everyone has a distinct purpose that serves as a compass in life. Whether walking dogs, collecting garbage, or excelling in physics, your role matters greatly. Embrace what you do with pride, as it adds value to the fabric of humanity. As we explore further, it's important to acknowledge that each person has their own unique perspective, yet we are all connected by shared goals. Understanding this allows us to take control of our futures and build genuine relationships beyond surface-level interactions.

In the quest for success, it's tempting to prioritize money and prestigious careers. However, it's worth taking a moment to reflect on the fact that everyone's path is different, and genuine satisfaction doesn't always come from pursuing the highest salary.

It's crucial to recognize the subtle nudges from the universe, the gentle whispers of Mother Nature guiding us toward our authentic paths. Picture this: you're striving toward a goal, yet obstacles seem to block your every move. These roadblocks aren't mere chance occurrences—they're messages urging you to reassess your direction.

When you encounter repeated hurdles, it's a sign to pause, reflect, and pivot if necessary. Money shouldn't be the sole determinant of your career path. Just as atoms find their place in the universe, we belong within certain circles, resonating with those who complement our skills and aspirations.

Consider a football team in perfect synergy—the tackle, the quarterback, the wide receiver, the running back—all functioning harmoniously. They anticipate each other's moves, achieving victories that seem effortless. In life, too, we must find our counterparts who elevate our endeavors to unparalleled heights.

Just as a symphony requires every instrument to play in harmony, your success is intricately tied to finding your tribe, your collaborators who amplify your strengths and propel you toward greatness. Remember, every setback is an opportunity to realign with your true purpose. Stay attuned to the whispers of the universe, and let them guide you toward your most authentic and fulfilling path.

In the grand scheme of things, every individual plays a vital role. Whether it's the visionary minds who conceive ideas, the skilled craftsmen who bring them to life, or the meticulous mathematicians who ensure their accuracy, each person contributes to the success of a venture. Even those who handle administrative tasks or perform janitorial duties are integral parts of the equation. It's the collective effort of these individuals that propels a company toward excellence.

It's essential to recognize that everyone has a purpose in life. No life is wasted unless it's squandered. Take a moment to reflect on what brings you pride and energy, what ignites your passion, and what fuels your drive. These are the guiding forces that sustain us through each day, especially when considering the trajectory of our careers over the next few decades.

Life's purpose lies in finding your unique path and contributing to the advancement of those around you. When faced with obstacles, it's okay to pause, reassess, or even backtrack until you find a clearer path forward. Remember, evolution is about growth and progress, both personally and professionally.

As we delve deeper into the chapters of life, we confront the concepts of heaven and hell. It's a reflection of our journey thus far, culminating in the realization that life extends beyond the confines of our earthly existence. With billions of lives lost throughout history, it's humbling to contemplate the vastness of the universe and the countless planets that may have experienced similar trials and tribulations.

In contemplating the afterlife, we must consider the possibility of existence beyond our earthly forms. Perhaps it's not a realm defined by familiar physical attributes but rather a continuation of consciousness and energy. By embracing this broader perspective, we acknowledge the interconnectedness of all life and the infinite possibilities that lie ahead.

As we wrap up this chapter, let's recall that life is about more than just us. It's about aiming for personal growth, finding fulfillment, and playing a part in the progress of humanity as a whole. Therefore, embrace your purpose, tackle obstacles, and keep evolving, recognizing that your journey is connected to a larger whole.

As you start tallying up those numbers, you realize how vast the potential is. Imagine a vast universe filled with life, free from pain and suffering. It might seem like a fairy tale, but as we examine the core of existence and delve into the interconnectedness of all beings, this notion becomes a reality.

Consider the humble atom, the building block of all matter. It's a network of particles held together by energy in its simplest form. From a piece of concrete to the air we breathe, everything around us is comprised of these minuscule balls dancing in an intricate web of energy. Zoom out, and you'd witness a cosmic symphony, countless spheres connected by an unfathomable amount of energy.

Now, here's where it gets truly fascinating. Those strands of energy that weave the fabric of our reality? They carry memories. Every experience and every emotion we encounter in this earthly existence is imprinted within us. And when our time here reaches its end, those cherished memories accompany us beyond the veil.

So, what's the key to crafting a heavenly existence? It's simple yet profound: connect and uplift others. Life is a precious gift, a chance for us to feel a range of emotions and grow. We should make the most of it by forming genuine connections and helping others. This benefits those around us and brings us fulfillment and satisfaction.

Love possesses immense power within the universe. Genuine, selfless love goes beyond mere emotions or physical bonds; it's about uplifting and supporting others. When you offer assistance to someone in need, you initiate a ripple effect that reaches far and wide, impacting the lives of numerous individuals.

Consider the impact of aiding 500 individuals throughout your life. Each person will hold onto the memory of your support and benevolence. They'll recount your acts of kindness to those close to them, ensuring that your legacy of goodness endures through time. In exchange, you'll be rewarded with a wealth of positive vibes and sincere appreciation tenfold or more.

Even after passing away, your influence persists. Memories and emotions endure, connecting beyond the boundaries of time and space. Though your body may no longer exist, your essence remains intertwined with the universe. You contribute to a collective memory where moments of happiness and connection with others endure.

Just like the strands of a spider web, our lives are connected by shared experiences and memories. Even in death, this connection persists, enabling us to reunite with loved ones and carry on our journey together.

We're all connected in life and beyond. Spread love and kindness and share knowledge. Each of us contributes to humanity's growth.

Let's tap into the knowledge we have gained from around the world and others to move forward positively. We aim for clean energy, peaceful resolutions, and a world without war. Together, we can build a better world driven by love, compassion, and human potential.

As you delve into the contents of this book, I aim for you to understand the core of my journey. It's about discovering yourself, evolving, and recognizing our ability to learn and connect profoundly. Whether through technology, music, mathematics, or just sharing experiences, we can exchange this vast knowledge and uplift one another.

The reason for sharing this knowledge extends beyond personal growth; it aims to contribute to the advancement of our surroundings. Evolution isn't confined to biology; it's fundamental to life. By embracing our individual viewpoints and capabilities, we foster positive change globally.

Each person has a counterpart, someone, or a group who shares their thoughts and passions. Differences shouldn't isolate us; instead, they make us unique. Embrace your differences, find your purpose, pursue your passions, and spread love and kindness. In doing so, you'll create your own version of heaven on Earth.

Be cautious of taking shortcuts or succumbing to temptations that can lead to negative outcomes. While material wealth, power, and status might provide momentary gratification, genuine fulfillment stems from a life marked by love, compassion, and integrity. Keep in mind that every choice we make has repercussions, not just in the present but also in the future.

Those who spread negativity and harm others may find themselves in a hell of their own making in the afterlife. Conversely, those who embody goodness and kindness will reap boundless rewards, mirroring the principles of cause and effect present on Earth in the heavens above.

Forgiveness plays a crucial role in freeing ourselves from the weight of past grievances and opening up to a brighter future. We make room for meaningful connections with others by releasing grudges and negative energy. In death, we surpass the constraints of our physical lives, becoming part of a larger network of souls who have traversed time and space alongside us.

As you finish reading this book, I trust you've acquired valuable insights that will stay with you even after you've finished it. Science serves not only as a field of study but also as a tool for comprehending the complexities of our world. Whether in our everyday actions or the vast scope of evolution, science provides clarity as we navigate our way forward.

Exploring our galaxy to uncover the wonders of other life forms is truly amazing. Life is a precious gift, and it's incredible to see how much progress we've made, all thanks to the guidance of science.

Science is the foundation of our comprehension of the universe, offering insights into its mysteries. It unveils the composition of all matter, from the smallest particles to the vastness of celestial bodies, revealing the common building blocks that shape reality: electrons, neutrons, and protons. However diverse we may seem, we're all linked on a fundamental level. Guided by universal principles, we interact with each other, each vibrating with life at different frequencies.

Exploring the domain of science reveals the complex relationship between frequency and energy. Resonance demonstrates how forces interact harmoniously, with the potential for both creation and destruction. Science enables us to anticipate and comprehend the mechanics of the universe, including planetary formation and stellar birth.

Think about the planets as simple particles coming together to create celestial bodies hanging in the enormous void of space. They, too, are governed by the same laws of nature, requiring energy to bind their constituent particles together. In this cosmic ballet, gravity emerges as the maestro, orchestrating the passage of time itself.

The notion that gravity birthed time itself is a profound one. Just like the universe originated from the Big Bang, time also had its inception. Time brings about change and evolution, propelling the ongoing story of existence.

Without evolution, stagnation ensues, leading ultimately to entropy and decay. Change is not just something we should want; it's something we need for growth and advancement. Accepting change is like embracing life because the core of vitality and rejuvenation lies in its constant movement. Let's begin this journey of self-discovery guided by the insights of science. By comprehending the universe, we gain insights into ourselves, and by accepting change, we uncover the core of our humanity.

Inertia, a pervasive force, impedes progress universally. Similar to gravity governing celestial movements, every aspect of our lives, regardless of scale, possesses significance and order.

Our discussions on the universe shed light on the creation of gravity – a frequency that pervades the cosmos, wielding both creative and destructive power. This understanding extends beyond the celestial realm to encompass our human experience. In our journey through the third chapter, we delved into spirituality, recognizing its profound influence on our lives.

Spirituality isn't limited to any specific group or belief system. It's a universal concept that goes beyond borders. When we embrace spirituality, we connect with a deeper sense of purpose and strength within ourselves. It's like being pulled toward something bigger, guiding us toward fulfillment and understanding of ourselves.

Thank you for joining me on this journey. I wish you days full of inspiration, growth, and endless opportunities. You have the ability to shape your future and heaven in the afterlife, making it one filled with love, hope, and endless potential. Believe in yourself and others, embrace what makes you unique, and let your light shine.